Ms Blaelock's Book of Minimally Viable Housekeeping

Also by Alexandria Blaelock

Ms Blaelock's Books
Stress Free Dinner Parties
Signature Wardrobe Planning
Holistic Personal Finance
Minimally Viable Housekeeping

Short Stories
Alma's Grace
Balancing the Book
Fate in Your Hands
Kiss of Death
Lady of the Looking Glass
Life in the Security Directorate
Long Weekend in the Snow
Love in the Security Directorate
Needy Bitch
Payton's Run
Phoenix Child
Shining Star
Ship in a Bottle
Simone Says Hands in the Air
The Guardian's Vigil
The Life and Death of Carmelita Basingstoke

Ms Blaelock's Book of Minimally Viable Housekeeping

Alexandria Blaelock

BlueMere Books
MELBOURNE, AUSTRALIA

Copyright © 2018 by Alexandria Blaelock.

All rights reserved. No part of this publication may be reproduced, distributed or transmitted in any form or by any means, including photocopying, recording, or other electronic or mechanical methods, without the prior written permission of the publisher, except in the case of brief quotations embodied in critical reviews and certain other non-commercial uses permitted by copyright law.

For permission requests, contact enquiries@bluemerebooks.com.

Ordering Information:
Discounts are available on quantity purchases. For details, contact orders@bluemerebooks.com.

Ms Blaelock's Book of Minimally Viable Housekeeping/Alexandria Blaelock.

hardback ISBN: 978-1-925749-02-1
paperback ISBN: 978-1-925749-01-4
digital ISBN: 978-1-925749-00-7

Book Layout © 2015 BookDesignTemplates.com
Cover Image © RetroClipArt/Shutterstock.com

Contents

Introduction 1
What is Housekeeping? 7
Why Do Housekeeping? 45
Who Does the Housekeeping? 55
When Does It Get Done? 67
Where Does it all Happen? 77
How: Getting It Done Effectively 89
How: Getting It Done Efficiently 99
Conclusion 123
Appendix A: For Those Working at Home 127
Appendix B: Housework Survey: What You Really Think. 137
Appendix C: Example Job Description 141
Glossary 145
Bibliography 147
Index 149
Author's Note 154
About the Author 155

With thanks to my husband, for:
- *Giving me the idea for this book, and*
- *Generally tolerating my lackadaisical housekeeping when I'm writing.*

One's philosophy is not best expressed in words; it is expressed in the choices one makes...

and the choices we make are ultimately our responsibility.

–ELEANOR ROOSEVELT

Introduction

IF YOU COULD SEE MY FACE, it would probably have the perpetual scowl of someone who is a full-time creative, full-time business operator, and full-time home manager. And I'm lucky - some have a fourth full-time job caring for their children or parents and some are full-time educators of their children too.

And somewhere in there we have to care for ourselves as well, or we'll go nuts, and there may be carnage. Or worse.

Perhaps you're one of the lucky ones, and your partner recognises the value of your non-home related jobs and puts their dirty underpants in the laundry hamper and their dishes in the dishwasher. But more likely, you're trying to juggle one or more paid jobs with a side gig/income producing hobby and still maintain some sort of order in your home.

It's bloody hard work.

You *are* a unique and special individual. I believe you were put on this Earth to do something magnificent. You might disagree, but whether you believe in a Deity's plan, or the randomness of evolution doesn't matter. There is only one of you, with your unique gifts and talents, and the opportunity to make this planet better than it is.

Having said that, maybe your magnificence is a well run and comfortable home. If so, this book is probably not for you. You should move onto advanced home management techniques like the psychology of comfort, interior design to nurture young brains or home care of the terminally ill.

Similarly, if you've a full-time housekeeping career running a hotel or some other kind of residential facility, you can move on too. Find a different type of continuous professional development program.

If, however, you're neck deep in activities related to one or more jobs and finding housework a time-sucking imposition you could do without, then you're in the right place.

Despite what most people think, historically speaking, it's only relatively recently that women's choices were reduced to marriage and staying home to care for their house and family. Yet even in today's "liberated" world, the background belief that a woman's place is in the home survives.

In some cases, the cost of replacing a housewife is so high many families have no option but for someone to stay at home. And with the gender pay disparity, that's usually the wife.

Even though some high-powered female executives would like a wife to take care of the housekeeping, it's more likely her partner feels it's best done by her. Regardless of the work she does, her hours or her income. Or how many breakfast meetings, networking events and late-night business deals she's responsible for.

And regardless of her income, she (and you) are guilt-ridden for not doing what you think is required of a "good" wife. And good, in this case, is both a general moral expectation and an indication of satisfactory performance.

So, how much does a good wife cost? Well, it depends on whether you're talking about her replacement cost (to buy all the services she undertakes), her opportunity cost (the loss you face without her), or compensation cost (for her death or disablement). And whether you're talking about the quantity or quality of her work.

It doesn't help that many people believe it's a woman's nature to care and nurture (as opposed to her circumstances making it necessary).

And following this, that women don't need formal education for it because they instinctively know how to care for their homes and families.

It took women like Catherine Beecher (1800 - 1878) and Ellen Richards (1842 - 1911) to push for formal domestic science education covering the basics of food and nutrition, budgeting, resource management and sewing. Not just at school, but university level too.

More recently, domestic science seems irrelevant in the face of technological changes including chemical cleaning products, ready-made meals, refrigerators, and dishwashers. We are once more thrown back to instinct and the assumption "mother knows best". Along with "cleanliness is next to godliness" and "women's work is never done".

I learnt about being a housewife during the 1970s and 80s. I learnt from my mother, who learnt from her mother during the 1930s and 40s. And my grandmother learned about housekeeping from her mother in the 1910s.

There's quite a lot of difference between Grannie's childhood home and mine - my great Grandpa worked in a coal mine, and they rented a cottage owned by the business nearby. Great Grannie cooked over an open fire and didn't have running water or electricity. She didn't go to school, couldn't read, didn't know anything about germs, only that hard work was her lot in life.

And to make matters worse, my parents thought a good education was critical for a better life, (I was the first to get a University qualification). They believed it was more important I spend time studying and preparing for University entrance exams than doing chores, so when I left home to live in student digs, I had no idea how to cook or clean. I more or less made it up as I went along. So much for instinct.

But like you, I'm sick of having that argument about who is and isn't pulling their weight in the housework department. It's time to cut the crap and figure out what is and isn't necessary, and how to get it over in the shortest possible time so I can get on with the activities I think make life worth living.

So, from here on, I'll be referring to housework as housekeeping because my *work* is writing and editing.

I ensure the tasks required to keep the house in a reasonable state get done - I *manage* the housekeeping, but I don't necessarily do it myself.

As a youngster in primary school, I learnt the basic 5W1H research/problem-solving technique, and this book applies that technique to housekeeping:

- **WHAT** exactly is this housekeeping of which you speak?
- That sounds boring, **WHY** do it?
- Okay maybe, but **WHO** does it?
- And **WHEN** does it get done?
- And **WHERE** does it all happen?
- But **HOW** does it all get done?

Minimally Viable Housekeeping

We'll look at each of these questions, figure out how they apply to you, and what your version of minimally viable housekeeping looks like. Which will be different to mine because we're not living the same life.

To help with this, I'm going to use the Julian Fellowes' TV series *Downton Abbey* to illustrate how the housekeeping got done in a late Victorian era country house.

You don't need to have seen the show because I'll explain the concepts, but if I mention Mrs Hughes or Mrs Patmore, it may be easier for you to understand what I am trying to say.

Downton Abbey is, of course, fiction and doesn't include a lot of everyday household activity, but it's a good representation nonetheless.

And for a little modern-day action, I'll compare this with hotel operations.

But before we get into the nitty-gritty, I'd like to warn you about what Christine Frederick (1883 - 1970) called "Competent Counsel".

She was a domestic scientist and advocate of scientific home management in the days when running water and electricity were only just becoming household realities.

She wrote books applying efficiency and productivity principles in the home but is mostly forgotten aside from academics (and me).

One of her tips I'm fond of is to make a comfortable place where you can rest (nap even) between heavy chores. A nest if you like - pets optional.

Anyway, Mrs Frederick argued there's no place for common sense in housekeeping, and housekeepers should stay up to date with the latest changes in technology and practices that could increase the comfort and ease of housekeeping.

For which, you take "competent counsel" (expert advice) from books, magazines, appliance manufacturers and government departments.

And while I agree you should stay up to date, and upgrade as appropriate, I also think you need to be a little critical (in the academic sense) of the advice given and question the source's credentials and motive:

- Is the magazine advising you on achieving a bum of Kardashian proportions, how to apply the latest smokey eye makeup, and please your partner in bed a credible source of housekeeping advice?

- What sort of commission arrangement does the vacuum cleaner salesperson work on, and does this affect the reliability of their advice?

- Is the scientist telling you to wash your towels every other day with antibacterial detergent, paid by the manufacturers of the laundry detergent? What kind of towels were they researching? What were the experiment parameters? Did the research relate to disease transfer in bathrooms or bacterial contamination of food or kitchen surfaces? Has the media misrepresented the outcome?

- Is the government department looking after consumer or other interests?

And for that matter, even me - while I want you to feel comfortable and in control of the housekeeping you do (and not feel guilty about what you don't), I also want you to buy my books, so I get a couple of bucks after I've had them made.

CHAPTER 1

What is Housekeeping?

WHEN I WAS THINKING ABOUT writing this book, I started asking people what they thought about housework and housekeeping. Not really surprisingly, no one knew what it is; most thought it was "just" cleaning. So, I asked a dictionary.

Definitions

Housekeeping

The Oxford English Dictionary defines housekeeping as *managing* household affairs. Housekeeping is also used to describe business operations that support productive work, and some biological processes; presumably the ones keeping us alive.

This notion of managing is important because managing is not the same thing as doing.

Minimally Viable

Now we know what housekeeping is, what's minimally viable?

It's the smallest possible thing that will satisfy demand.

- A Minimal Viable Product consists of just enough practicality to satisfy purchasers. It might be a crappy second-rate product that's not worth developing further for a higher paying audience, but that doesn't matter. It is what it is, and that's just enough.

- Your Minimal Viable Income covers your basic living costs. Of course, you want more, but it meets your needs. It's just enough.

- The Minimum Viable Effort is the least possible amount of work an employee has to do to not get fired. It might be enough today, but if you don't keep developing your skills, it might not be enough tomorrow.

Minimally Viable Housekeeping

Minimally viable housekeeping is the least possible *necessary* housework. It's the essential stuff that must be done, even on the messiest kind of day which disappears, leaving your breakfast dishes on the kitchen counter, your clean clothes stagnating in the washing machine, and even worse, your dinner still in the freezer. (Ooh - let me just get something out for tea).

The minimum varies from person to person; you and your live-in partner (if you have one) need to decide what it is for your home. Particularly where your partner is the one who leaves the house to earn the money that puts the food in the freezer in the first place.

They might think it's a reasonable expectation that your part of the bargain involves clean toilets, ironed shirts in the wardrobe, and hot dinners on the table.

But the fact they're the breadwinner doesn't relieve them of all household responsibility, so it's good to synchronise expectations, regardless of the difficulty of the conversation.

Housekeeping Duties

Now, as you know, I'm a writer, so I know words have power. So, before we move on, let's take a look at the difference between professional and amateur housekeepers.

Professional Housekeepers

For a start, professional housekeepers get paid!

When you take a job housekeeping for someone else, you get a job description that describes what to do, and how you'll do it. Let's use a hotel maid as an example.

> **Purpose:** to maintain a clean, sanitary, comfortable and tidy environment.

Responsibilities/Duties: (what hotel owners expect) protect hotel property, keep guests happy, and comply with policies and procedures.

Knowledge/Experience/Capability: (what you need to meet your employer's expectations) understands cleaning products, techniques and methods. The physical stamina and mobility to bend, reach, kneel, and push/pull 15 kg (33 lbs) through the day.

Competencies: (generic abilities you need to meet your employer's expectations) customer focus, attention to detail, and honesty.

Tasks: (defined pieces of work) distribute linen, towels and room supplies using wheeled carts, restock room supplies (drinking glasses, soaps, shampoos, writing supplies, mini bar), and check all room appliances are in working order.

Hours of Work: (expected time commitment) for example, full or part-time, nights, weekends, on call.

Amateur Housekeepers

Whether they are enthusiastic or not, amateur housekeepers are unpaid and untrained.

They don't have information to help them get the job done. Nor do they have a purpose, tasks, or responsibilities. They don't think about the policies, procedures, knowledge or competencies they need, and for the most part, they don't think about restricting the amount of time they spend on the job.

Instead, they do chores.

Chores are torturous things your parents made you do; you might make yours do some too. Some kids get pocket money, and spend it on lollies. (Mmmmm - chocolate mint balls).

You were never entirely sure what "tidy your room" meant, all you knew was you were confined to it until your Mum was satisfied with the results which generally meant you were stuck in there for hours and hours and hours (if not days)! And she still wasn't happy.

Keeping House in the Big House

Managing household affairs may not make much sense to you in your modern life, so let's do a bit of history and look at an early twentieth century household through the historical drama *Downton Abbey*.

These are the roles you undertake in your somewhat smaller home, and need to consider when you're thinking in terms of minimally viable.

Lady Cora (Wife and Mother, has an interest in smooth home operations)

Cora Levinson was an American dry goods heiress. Her social climbing mother took her to London with the specific goal of marrying her off to an impoverished British nobleman (in the end Robert Crawley, Earl of Grantham) in exchange for an estate saving fortune.

As Countess, her primary function is to produce legitimate heirs (sons), and while she gave birth to three daughters, she failed to provide a son.

However, she was a loving wife and mother, and openly cared very deeply for her family, perhaps more than was socially acceptable at the time.

In the event of her death, it's possible Robert would marry again, there would be a second Lady Grantham who could potentially produce an heir. But there would never be another Cora - she is irreplaceable.

Lady Cora employs Mrs Hughes to manage the household operations on her behalf.

Mrs Hughes (Housekeeper)

Mrs Hughes represents Lady Cora outside the confines of the family, including to the servants.

She takes care of the relevant family business during the day but retires to her private rooms in the evening. Her hours are not explicit in the show, but she'd have time off, perhaps a half day each week and a whole day each month.

As an unmarried woman, she's called Mrs in deference to her position as the most senior female servant, in charge of household operations:

- Scheduling the daily and seasonal work of the staff.
- Household cleaning, plus maintaining fixtures and appliances.
- Dressmaking and laundry.
- Reviewing and ordering supplies.
- Paying bills, reconciling the household accounts, and managing the records.
- Supervising female staff.

If you've watched the show, you'll know that even though she's responsible for keeping the house(s) operating efficiently, she does very little physical labour.

Her job is to tell people what to do and make sure they have the resources they need when they need them. She's more of an organiser than a doer; a manager in fact.

She delegates the cooking to Mrs Patmore, cleaning to Head Housemaid Anna Smith (who later marries Mr Bates and is promoted to Lady Mary's Lady's Maid - try saying that five times fast), and laundry to an unmentioned Head Laundress.

While the family are fond of her and decide to keep her on (instead of dismissing her) when she marries Carson, she will at some point be forced to retire and be replaced by a new housekeeper.

Carson (Butler)

Carson is the most senior staff member; the head or chief of staff. He's in charge of the dining room, the pantry (where the silverware, crystal and other expensive items are kept), the wine cellar and male staff. Most of us know him for his role opening the door at which point he becomes a sort of security guard come bouncer.

You undertake versions of these tasks, but:

- Modern silverware comes with anti-tarnish coatings, and you can have old silver re-coated. Though you probably don't have silverware, and even if you did, you probably wouldn't clean it regularly anyway.

- Crystal isn't dishwasher safe, so even if you own some, it's unlikely you use it.

- If you buy alcohol, it's probably part of your regular grocery shopping. You might want a wine cellar that serves hundreds, but don't have the space for it.

- You don't think of serving food as a "thing" because you don't have to get it more than a dozen steps from your kitchen. You're not trying to coordinate half a dozen footmen keeping it hot on its way from the downstairs kitchen to the upstairs dining room.

- You answer your own door on the rare occasions anyone knocks on it.

So, having acknowledged Carson, we'll be leaving him here and not talking about butlering in your own home any further.

Mrs Patmore (Cook)

Mrs (by courtesy) Patmore runs the kitchen and is responsible for feeding family and domestic staff; all to a set schedule. You might recall the episode she has a mini-meltdown because her schedule was blown and she couldn't keep the food fresh.

She prepares the daily and special event menus in consultation with Lady Cora but works closely with Mrs Hughes to order and pay for equipment and supplies.

She supervises the kitchen staff who maintain the kitchen equipment, do the dishes, monitor and maintain food supplies. Her practical planning ensures the maximum benefit of supplies on hand and minimal waste through spoilage.

Miss Smith (Head Housemaid)

I'm calling the Head Housemaid Miss Smith because the series doesn't mention who replaces her when she is promoted to Lady's Maid.

She's responsible for cleaning, serving afternoon tea, ensuring the fires are well stoked, the lighting adequate, fetching items for the family, emptying chamber pots.

She does get "hands on", but her primary task is to manage the housemaids, and a big house would have many assorted maids including scullery, kitchen, chamber, and parlour. You can probably guess the scullery maid worked in the scullery, and the chambermaid in the bedrooms and so on.

Lady's Maid (Baxter)/Valet (Bates)

These roles involve the intimate personal care of the family;

- Assisting with bathing, shaving, hair setting, and dressing. Also purchasing and maintaining toilet articles such as brushes, shaving gear, and related products such as fragrances or skin care.

- Keeping the bedroom clean, tidy, and comfortable (not doing it themselves, but ensuring the chambermaid does a satisfactory job).

- Caring for clothing: purchasing, altering, and mending them before sending them to the laundry. Ensuring they're in good repair before putting them back in the wardrobe. Cleaning very fine or delicate items.

- Making travel arrangements and packing appropriate clothing.

Nanny/Governess/Tutor

While titled parents probably loved their children a great deal, they were also committed to keeping up appearances. They would leave the estate for long periods of time to attend functions/court in town and needed people to take care of the children left behind.

Nanny is a paid staff member, but as she works very closely with the family, she is not considered a servant. She almost exclusively cares for the children until they are old enough to start their schooling. And when I say caring, I mean all of it; feeding, bathing, dressing, entertaining, and putting them to bed. Plus, some repair and manufacture of clothing.

The Governess (for girls) or Tutor (for boys) took care of the child's primary education until they were old enough to go to boarding school, finishing school, university, or the marriage market.

As girls grew older, the Governess would also act as a chaperone, ensuring the young woman's reputation remained clear.

Some Governesses stayed on at the house after the girls were married as a companion or secretary for the Lady of the house.

Head Laundress

So far as I can recall, *Downton Abbey* doesn't mention how the laundry gets done.

But the Head Laundress assigns tasks (sorting, soaking, bleaching, washing, drying, starching, and ironing) to the Laundry maids or sends it out where necessary.

She launders only the most delicate and valuable items. As well as keeping the laundry rooms and tools clean, she's responsible for ensuring the house has clean clothes and linens.

Estate Manager (Branson)

Downton Abbey concerns the house and the people who live and work within it; the garden is just a beautiful backdrop to intense conversations between the characters.

As far as the house is concerned, Mrs Hughes' outdoor responsibilities only extend as far as meeting the indoor needs.

But the land was a critical component of Great House operations, and we start to see this when Branson takes over the role of Estate Manager.

He becomes responsible for generating farm income, providing food for the table, and maintaining impressive recreational and leisure areas.

Again, he doesn't do it all himself, he has the Head Gardener, Stable Master, and Gamekeeper to help.

General Thoughts on Big House staffing

Downton Abbey is filmed at Highclere Castle; the 30 square foot house sits in 6,000 acres of land and contains about 300 rooms. Its present-day staff complement ranges between 60 - 150 staff. Some are permanent, and the rest are seasonal workers over the tourist season.

Admittedly, your home is unlikely to be at this scale, but you can see you may be performing the work of eight full-time roles, plus their staff too.

Each servant had to complete their full to-do list every day, and if it came about they couldn't, they generally found themselves unemployed.

The Housekeeper may have made a case for additional staff as the household changed and the amount of work increased, but changes would probably take months to come to fruition.

Domestic staff were cheap and easy to find before the First World War, but it was much harder after. Partly because there just weren't enough people, and partly because factories, offices and shops offered shorter hours, higher pay and less gruelling work.

You get a small taste of this in Downton Abbey when Gwen Dawson quits her job as a maid to become a secretary, and Thomas Barrow seeks a position as Butler.

Keeping House in a Hotel

Hotel hierarchy is similar to the big house - though, in a large hotel, the Housekeeper may be known as something like the Director of Operations or Guest Services Manager. They are second in charge reporting to the hotel's General Manager.

Executive Housekeeper

Like Mrs Hughes, the Executive Housekeeper is responsible for getting it all done. As well as supervising the staff, they schedule cleaning, coordinate guest requests, monitor supplies and control the budget.

In a large establishment, the Executive Housekeeper may have an Assistant. They're a cross between a Second-in-Charge and an Executive Assistant, depending on the hotel size.

Managers

Managers are responsible for the cleanliness and smooth operations of their departments.

- The Public Area Manager is responsible for the cleanliness and safety of public areas such as the lobby, public bathrooms, and hallways.

- Floor Managers ensure guest rooms are clean, serviced, and the amenities replenished.

- The Control Desk Manager handles communications between the rooms and other departments, and ensures guest requirements are met. They schedule cleaning, maintain records of cleaning activities, and ensure there are sufficient supplies and equipment to complete the work.

- The Laundry Manager ensures the ongoing supply of clean towels and bedding. The may also coordinate cleaning of guest clothing.

Attendants

Each Manager supervises a team of attendants. Like the housemaids, they have areas of focus; depending on who they report to, that could be public areas, guest rooms or laundry.

Food and Beverages

In smaller hotels, food provision reports through the Executive Housekeeper. Larger hotels usually have an Executive at the same level reporting directly to the General Manager.

Minimally Viable Housekeeping

General Thoughts on Hotel Staffing

I know modern day hotel operations seem more abstract than a fictional aristocratic house of the Edwardian era. Perhaps because we know there is an army of workers in there everyday bustling around cleaning. After all, if you've visited a hotel, even for just a few hours, you've seen them.

And perhaps the sleek professionalism of their uniforms and carts makes what they do seem more remote from what you do than it really is.

For your minimally viable housekeeping, you should aim at the slick and efficient end of the spectrum. Then you can hang up your apron, put your cart away and become Lady Cora enjoying the things that make your life worth living.

Keeping House in Your Small Home

Cleaning is just part of the housekeeping equation. There's also cooking, child and pet care, shopping, and running errands.

Plus, organising services like plumbers to fix the drains, coordinating the maintenance, repair, and replacement of fixtures and fittings like hot water and climate control systems.

Not to mention, taking care of the paperwork: paying bills, making sure the insurance is up to date, the mortgage gets paid, and the credit cards aren't overextended.

But when most of us think about housekeeping, what we generally think about is just the cleaning.

So, let's *Downton Abbey* your home.

Housekeeping

As well as the physical component, there's the mental component of thinking, planning, paying the bills and doing the filing. You'll need an "office" or "command centre", even if it's just a small, quiet and private space where you've a reasonable chance of not being interrupted.

It should be equipped with a desk or table and chair, a shelf for your paperwork, a box for your records, and a little cash just in case. Maybe a couch for naps.

You could also keep some hand cream handy, plus a damp cloth and a mirror in case you want to freshen up when someone knocks on the door.

Planning, Scheduling and Dispatching

As the Housekeeper, you're now an executive as well as a labourer; you're managing the tasks as well as doing some or all of them. The executive functions of planning, scheduling and dispatching tasks may be more important because they not only ensure the tasks get done, but done efficiently.

Planning

One of the most important things you'll do is make plans to ensure the right tasks get done at the right time.

Planning them ensures they're completed efficiently, on a schedule that's not too tight or too loose, with the right tools in the right place. It keeps you focused, reduces decision fatigue, and eases the formation of regular habits.

Poorly planned tasks are either not done well, or not done at all; perhaps there is insufficient time, or the right tools and supplies aren't available. Or maybe you're just not sure what needs to be done next.

It's like when you're watching a movie, and everything is in chaos, and no one has any idea what to do. Until someone steps up and says "here's the plan" and you know it's going to work out. Then they explain, step by step; which character has to do what by when so all the characters can do their parts, so the good guys can win.

Minimally Viable Housekeeping

Of course, to have a plan, you need to know what the end result is going to be. Whether that's clean bathroom, a hot meal on the table, or getting the bills paid. Plus, you need to know when you need that clean bathroom, hot meal or bill paid.

For example, you may want your climate control system to reliably heat and cool your home without killing you in the process. Knowing that, you need to ensure it's regularly serviced and maintained so it doesn't break down, or spew contaminants such as bacteria or toxins into your home. And if you know the manufacturer gives it a 10-year warranty, then you need to start thinking about replacing it after nine years.

If you don't plan this, when it does break down, you'll have to spend time arranging repairs and dealing with the fallout. You'll be rushing your research and might not install the best available replacement system at that time.

And it's not just your equipment, but other tasks like repainting your window trim, cleaning and replacing your carpets, or replenishing your bed linens as well.

On a shorter timeframe, in a different department, planning your meals allows you to:

- Include all the food groups in their proper proportions (promoting good health).

- Purchase all the ingredients in the correct amounts ahead time (saving time, money and stress).

- Prepare quick or slow-cooked meals according to the demands on your time (scheduling).

- Identify and take advantage of multi-tasking efficiencies (dispatching).

And while we're on the subject of planning, it's worth taking the time to think through a Contingency Plan or Plan B in case you're unable to take care of the tasks for some reason.

If you've prepared an action plan, your partner doesn't have to stress about it - they just start with step one. For example, call your mother to take care of the kids, get your prepared meals from the freezer, or call ACME Home Care to clean up.

Scheduling

Scheduling is the critical part of planning, it's deciding when the various components of a job such as "Clean Garage" get done. If you don't have or use a schedule, you're usually trying to get more done each day than is actually possible.

With a schedule, you can distribute tasks evenly throughout your week according to the needs of your household. For example, if you've just had a baby, you'll need to organise around feeding times. Or if you only have access to a car one day a week, that's when you go shopping and run your other errands. And if you iron, it's probably after washing.

Your schedule guides your ordinary every day. It helps to prevent tasks building up to seemingly insurmountable levels and keeps you focused on your core daily priorities.

At times, circumstances will seemingly conspire to prevent you sticking to your schedule. It doesn't matter what happens, you can still follow your schedule, but choose to start earlier, finish later or reschedule tasks for another day.

If you happen to notice that something needs doing, you can choose whether to do it then and there, or add it to the schedule for another day.

Knowing what needs to be done, and that you're in control of it provides a tremendous sense of comfort. And just as if you were working in that hotel, reminds you to take breaks, include rest periods to protect your physical and mental wellbeing, and balance hard labour with light to manage fatigue.

Your overall schedule is made up of tasks that take place on different frequencies; daily, weekly, monthly, seasonal (e.g., swapping seasonal wardrobes), irregular (e.g., planning a trip), and "special projects" like getting a plumber in to deal with the blocked drains.

Some follow a "necessary" schedule, (e.g., planning meals before shopping), some are more logical, (e.g., cleaning from the top down), yet others follow the flow of your week (e.g., vacuuming on Fridays, so the house looks neat and clean for the weekend).

Plus, there are frequent but unpredictable tasks, like emptying the bins or shopping that take place in the context of other jobs. And projects with defined starts, finishes, and sometimes deadlines.

Daily tasks are predictable to an extent because you've meals to provide, children to care for, and dogs to walk. You'll probably be interrupted, but can schedule focused jobs (e.g., baking) for times you're reasonably sure will be uninterrupted, (e.g., baby's nap time). And when you expect interruptions, (e.g., you're waiting for the plumber) you can plan less intensive tasks like tidying up and putting things away.

Plus, you'll need a bring forward system (e.g., tickler file, to-do list or calendar) to keep your seasonal and irregular tasks front of mind.

Remember to keep your schedule simple and manageable - it's a means to an end, not an end in itself.

Dispatching

Once you've set a schedule, you can dispatch your tasks without interruption. Dispatching involves allocating time and resources to each task, taking into account all the jobs you need to complete. Like a train moving from station to station, or when a company is doing quotes in your area and calls to offer you an appointment.

It might seem at first glance that you've no need for dispatching, but if we call it "delegating", you might understand it better. As well as managing your own tasks, you'll be delegating them to your partner and children, and at times, organising trades or services to do others.

At which point it becomes more apparent that smooth operation is a matter of properly dispatching the task process. Efficient dispatch relies on the exact arrangement of equipment in its own place, and that tools and supplies are returned to theirs when they are no longer needed. The easiest way to lose time and momentum in dispatching is to run out of supplies or not be able to find your tools.

Remember, the goal of dispatching is to reduce labour, not guarantee quality. Use all the equipment and efficient methods you need to reduce the drudgery, and ensure you're not left exhausted by the demands of your day.

Purchasing

These days you're more likely to consume purchased goods than home grown or made, so your focus will be making responsible values and standards-based purchasing decisions.

These decisions rely on knowing a bit about the goods:

- **Nutrition:** you can confidently buy less expensive food with the same or higher nutritional value. Plus, you can get different types of food to ensure a varied diet at a manageable cost. When you buy processed food, you'll know whether the products have too much salt, sugar, colourings, or preservatives. You'll also know whether your jar of tomato sauce is mostly tomato or something else.

- **Food Handling:** you can avoid stores, restaurants, and purchases that might make you ill.

- **Food Storage:** enables you to store products for long-term freshness and viability as well as pest deterrence.

- **Product Lifespan:** you can make well-informed choices about bulk purchasing - exactly how long does it take you to use up a container of coffee?

- **Fabrics:** you can choose clothing with appropriate durability, quality, and care requirements. You'll also have an idea about whether the price is about right for the garments.

- **Time and Effort to Clean Your Home:** helps you choose home decorations you have the time and inclination to care for. And dispose of the ones you aren't willing to care for.

Not to mention, that you can

- Save money and reduce purchasing mistakes.

- Balance price and value better.

- Shop seasonally and in the sales to take advantage of the low cost of oversupplies and avoid the high cost of shortages.

- Decide whether a subscription service is the right solution for you.

- Avoid waste.

Accounts

Sadly, you can't avoid paying the bills, so you need a plan for:

- Knowing when they need to be paid,

- Having money available to pay them, and

- Knowing when they've been paid.

You can't accurately plan for this unless you maintain records of income and expenditure to provide a basis for estimating the cost of running your household.

Generally, this process is called bookkeeping or accounts. For it to function correctly, you need a spending plan (or budget), but the spending plan won't work unless you keep accounts! Your accounts tell you where the money's going, but it's your spending plan gives you the opportunity to manage it.

Mrs Hughes kept an account book with columns for expenditure items and rows for the date. Purchases were entered in the book and totalled monthly, or when the bills were due. The budget would be reconciled by deducting expenditure from income, and the cash on hand counted to ensure that it equalled that amount.

The value of the account book approach is you can see where your money is going, and what areas can be cut back. By comparing a single item against the total expenditure, you can get a feel for whether it's costing too great a proportion of your income for the return you get on it.

You can also get an idea of how your expenses change month to month, and while it's fresh in your mind determine the reasonableness of the cost, as well as take an average across a period or examine the variations. It may also give you information about where your household leaks money.

You could use an app instead of a book, but the main thing is to keep it up to date.

Managing your household finances is critical to running your home well, and ensuring happy relationships within it. This relies on agreements between you and your partner about how the money is to be used. Clearly, there will be unhappiness if one saves and the other spends.

Record Keeping

A record is just a piece of information that needs to be preserved for a period of time. That might be a purchase receipt until the warranty expires, your spectacle prescription until it changes, or your tax return for the statute of limitations.

Your record management process starts when you receive a record. You have to:

- Decide what action to take, like, pay the bill.

- Schedule the action; bill paying day next Thursday.

- Perform the action; pay the bill and note evidence of completion; such as date and receipt number.

- Determine how long to keep the record; until the next bill comes in, or for a year of monitoring.

- Transfer the record to long-term storage; scan and store electronically, or place in a filing cabinet.

- Remove and destroy records according to the schedule you devise.

Every household is different, so every set of records has different requirements - you get to set up your system the way that's best for you.

If you don't have a system, you can waste a lot of time and effort trying to find the record you need. Not just bills and credit card statements, but vaccination certificates, recipes, or even clothing.

A consistent process and storage system solves this problem. It sounds complicated and time-consuming, but it's the system that makes information retrieval quick and easy.

You might choose to include categories for:

- **Friends and Family:** addresses, birthdays, anniversaries, spouse and children's names, memberships and interests, gifts given and received, clothing sizes, where off-season clothes are stored and so on.

- **Medical:** Practitioners, medications, test results, vaccinations, surgeries, spectacle prescriptions, dental fillings and the like.

- **Household:** Purchases, repairs, maintenance and disposals, room sizes, paint and wallpaper estimates, colours/papers used. Linen costs and replacement schedule. Pantry contents and replenishment. Inventory of your home contents; purchase dates, serial numbers, maintenance records (for insurance).

- **Financial:** Account books, income, taxes, insurances, bank records, safety deposit box locations and contents, real estate, bills due and paid, and so on.

- **Personal:** Letters, clippings, handy hints and tips you might follow up one day.

- **Libraries/collections:** Books, music, movies, comics, collectibles, crafts.

- **Trades/Services:** Contacts, operating hours.

- **Emergency:** Treatments and contacts for conditions you're managing

Cooking

While you can skip the cleaning, you can't skip food provision.

Going back to Mrs Patmore, you're in charge of producing 21 meals each week. It might be that you plan, purchase, cook, serve and clean up. Or you might take the family out for burgers, or have pizza delivered.

Minimally Viable Housekeeping

You could just feed your family, but you'll all be healthier and happier if you try to balance your nutritional needs, provide a variety of flavours and textures, and create a comfortable, stress-free environment to sit down and eat in.

A lot has changed in this area too. You probably aren't raising or slaughtering your food; you can access fresh ingredients jetted in from around the world, neatly packaged and shelved at your local supermarket.

You don't have to think about how to prepare an entire carcass before it starts rotting, and in fact, you may find it difficult to get half a side of beef or even a whole chicken!

Plus, you can buy your coffee ground and roasted, or ready-made so all you need to do is add hot water!

You also have a range of electronic appliances that can help you quickly and easily prepare food. Like, whip up cake batter in a matter of minutes rather than laboriously beating by hand with a wooden spoon. Or a couple of minutes in the microwave rather than a hot oven for an hour.

And for that matter, not having to keep an eye on the fire to ensure it doesn't go out before your cake is cooked!

Cleaning

According to the Oxford English Dictionary, clean is a word of many meanings.

It can be an adjective (describing word) meaning:

- Free from dirt.

- Morally uncontaminated (pure or innocent).

- Free from irregularities; having a smooth edge or surface.

- Giving a clear and distinctive impression to the senses; sharp and fresh.

It can be an adverb (changes the meaning of other words):

- To be free from dirt.
- To emphasise the completeness of a reported action, condition, or experience.

A verb (doing word):

- To remove dirt.

A noun (naming word):

- The act of cleaning something.

It's also used informally to describe

- Defeating or beating someone (cleaning someone's clock).
- Eliminating corruption or inefficiency (cleaning house).
- The absence of restraint (clean sheet or slate).
- Behaving better (cleaning up your act).
- Honesty (come clean).
- To be blameless (have clean hands).
- Not getting involved in illegal/immoral activities (keeping your hands clean).
- Confession (make a clean breast).
- Be thorough (do a clean job).
- Remove bad influences and prepare to start fresh, or win everything (clean sweep).
- Take all someone's money (clean out).

- Make a huge profit, or win everything or restore order (clean up).

That's quite a lot of pressure on five small letters, isn't it?

With the moral overtones of goodness and purity, it's easy to see how cleanliness can become an obsession, but it just means the absence/removal of dirt.

You don't *have* to get all Lady Macbeth about it.

Light v Deep v Spring Cleaning

I haven't been able to discover when cleaning became light or deep. Nor have I found a consistent definition of either.

What I have discovered, is that light cleaning is different from regular cleaning, and deep cleaning is not the same thing as Spring cleaning. So, if cleaning isn't bad enough, you now have to contend with four types of cleaning.

In my Great-Granny's day of dirt floors, wood or coal heating and cooking, oil lamps and wells, there was only cleaning. It was hard manual labour, and it took all day. Every day.

It's not really that long ago either. As recently as the 1950s, some women's lives were only a small step up from that.

In the old days, there was Spring cleaning. As the weather warmed up, you'd air out the house and give it a good clean.

This was necessary because as the weather cooled, you'd start closing rooms off from regular use and retreat to the warmest room in the house. And the warmest room was generally, the wood or coal-fired kitchen.

As the house shut down, the soot from the fire and lamps accumulated on surfaces. It was too cold to bathe as thoroughly, and many people would stop visiting the outhouse.

Nowadays we don't need to retreat to the kitchen for the winter. Electricity provides constant climate control year-round and running water the ability to bathe and toilet daily (we're so lucky).

This means you don't *need* to do a big annual clean, you can manage with regular, consistent activity.

Having said that, you might vacuum your carpets once a week, but have them cleaned every year or two depending on the size of your family, how many pets, and the quality of deposits they leave on the carpets.

It seems to me that the main difference between light and deep cleaning takes us back to the morality of cleanliness.

Deep cleaning requires a higher level of physical effort, for example, *dusting* is light, but *scrubbing* is deep.

It also requires a higher level of sanitation, so not just mopping the floors, but disinfecting them too (a two-step process).

I'm exhausted just typing it, let alone doing it.

Family Care

Aside from buying and maintaining clothing, your duties as Lady's Maid/Valet are probably quite limited unless you're caring for sick or elderly relatives.

This will be a difficult thing for you and your partner to negotiate with your ageing relatives, especially if they will be dependent on you for some or all of their care.

You can manage a lot of it by arranging services to regularly clean their homes, deliver food and take care of the laundry as well as irregular and ad hoc care. Which just leaves the question of who's going to pay for it.

If your parents or in-laws move into your home, they may not be happy about being dependent on you or helping out around the house or with the kids.

Similar issues will apply if you and your family leave your home and move into theirs.

All in all, this is a highly specialised area, and there is a lot of information and guidance out there so I won't be dealing with this in any detail.

I'll just say that you need to take care of yourself and draw lines between your role as a loving family member, and unpaid domestic servant.

Child Care

If you're primarily responsible for childcare, you probably don't need me to tell you how to do it. And if you do, then my advice is to look for someone who knows what they're talking about when it comes to childcare.

The only advice I can offer is to go with the flow and where possible, manage the other aspects of housekeeping around the needs of your children.

Pet Care

Pets need to be fed, taught how to behave amongst humans, and have their health maintained. They're unlikely to grow into creatures that pull their weight in the household (aside from the unconditional love that we all crave), so I'll only touch on them lightly.

Laundry

In the old days, laundry was a day of backbreaking torture, but now we lucky Western Women have running water and electricity. Something like washing clothes that used to take all day (plus another for ironing) takes an hour in the machine.

You don't have to carry and heat buckets of water, wash each garment individually in caustic cleaning solutions, beat them with sticks to get the dirt out or wring them to dry by hand. You also don't have to risk injury or allergy - your machine takes care of all that.

Another benefit of modernity is that most water is treated to kill bacteria and other life forms, as well as filtered and conditioned before it gets to the house.

You probably don't need to worry about managing the levels of lime, magnesium, or iron in the water, but if you do, you'll get better results if you mix your conditioning agents into the water before the soap and clothes.

Despite, or perhaps because of our fast and efficient modern appliances, I think that doing the laundry takes more time than any other task.

Modern mass production in underdeveloped countries has made clothes so cheap we don't feel the need to protect them with aprons or overalls let alone care enough to preserve them for the long haul. Not to mention that cleaning them is so quick and easy we tend to wash them more frequently.

And when those cheap clothes come out of the wash stained, or warped, or damaged, we just discard them and buy more cheap clothing to replace them.

Estate Management

Your estate management role will mainly consist of taking care of your car(s) and outdoor space, whether that's a small balcony or some land.

Garden/Yard Maintenance

I include garden because those of us with houses generally have gardens or some kind of open space that forms part of your property. You might use it to grow vegetables, you might have a collection of derelict cars, or it might be a jungle that's part of your strategic home defence plan.

You may not be the one that keeps it; your neighbour may strategically poison parts of it for you, someone else in your household may take care of it, or you might hire a service. But regardless of who does it, you'll be stopping it from getting in the house, cleaning up after it when it does, and maintaining features like swimming pools.

Self-care

Self-care is another activity that gets caught up in the morality debate, but let's not confuse it with vanity.

If you're a professional housekeeper, your employer is obliged by law to take care of your health and safety - to ensure that you aren't harmed or killed at work.

It's in their best interests too, because safe workplaces are generally efficient and productive ones. And if you're injured, they must pay for your treatment, or compensate you if you lose the capacity to work.

However, you're operating alone in your home, so the onus is on you to take your health and safety as seriously. Self-care is your version of occupational health and safety.

Let's take a look at your hands as an example. Each contains 27 bones, 29 joints, 123 ligaments, 48 nerves, and 30 arteries along with the muscles you need to manipulate them to pick up, move, and let go of all the items you deal with each day.

Along with that, you immerse them in water and a variety of cleaning chemicals as you complete your tasks. They're also exposed to surfaces and substances that are hot, cold, rough, sharp and slick. Every day you risk cuts, grazes, blisters, burns, bites, fractures, amputations, allergic reactions, crushing and electric shock. And this is not an exhaustive list.

Taking care of your hands is not vanity. Not only do you need to make sensible protective precautions (e.g., wearing the right glove for the job), you should consider proactive treatment options such as manicures as well.

Some will think a manicure is the height of selfish indulgence, but there are functional benefits. The hand massage increases blood flow, joint mobility and muscle flexibility. Adequately moisturised hands are less prone to cracking, sores and scarring. The chance of nail infection is reduced, and smooth snag free nails won't catch on or scratch items. There's also an element of stress reduction and relaxation which are useful for mood and attitude.

You deserve a safe and healthy workplace just like everyone else. A manicure might not be the thing for you, but perhaps a massage to help work out the kinks in your back. Or a bright pair of wellingtons for working in the garden. Maybe a high-quality hot chocolate mix for your afternoon slump

Risk Management

The critical element of protecting your health and safety is identifying and systematically managing risks.

1. Identify hazards with the potential to cause harm. They come from your environment, the tools and substances you use, and how you perform your tasks. The easiest way to identify them is to think of all the things that could go wrong and cause you injury. Like falling off a ladder when you're washing your second-floor windows.

2. Assess the risk of harm and the seriousness of the consequences. If you fall off the ladder, you could split your head open, dislocate your shoulder, or roll and come away unharmed.

3. Take action to control the risks. While we'd all like to think we'll get away injury free, it's more likely you'll get hurt. You might require hospitalisation, physical therapy, or suffer ongoing pain for the rest of your life. I expect you'd like to avoid that.

Risk controls come in a hierarchy from highest protection to lowest - you choose the most appropriate level to deal with the risk, ideally at the higher end of the hierarchy. Let's use falling off the ladder as an example again:

1. Eliminate the hazard. For example, get a professional service to wash the windows.
2. Substitute the hazard with something else; fix a ladder to the side of your house.
3. Reduce the risk through engineering controls; hire a scissor lift.
4. Reduce exposure with administrative controls; commonly by developing policies, standard practices, training or signage. You could choose to attend a course and use what you've learned to make further changes to your window cleaning process.
5. Use Personal Protective Equipment; it offers an additional barrier between you and the hazard, in this case, a hard hat, thick work clothes and boots.

Some of these controls (e.g., hiring a service) are more practical than others (hiring a scissor lift with appropriate fall restraints and arrests could be more expensive).

Others (attaching a ladder to the side of your house) are problematic for a range of non-safety related reasons (e.g., it would probably look really ugly) and are therefore unlikely.

You're more likely to manage any given risk with a combination of controls.

Once you've applied your controls, you need to review them to make sure they're effective. Not by throwing yourself off the ladder, but analysing the changes to see whether they create any new risks you need to deal with or if you're okay with the level of leftover risk.

Safety Policy

Having thought about your risks, it's worth developing a safety policy. Which sounds diabolical, but just lays out how you're going to practice your self-care. As your own employer, you've the freedom to include some options (like manicures) which wouldn't be offered by a hotel to its staff as a matter of course.

Scheduling

Earlier in the chapter, I mentioned balancing hard and light tasks, but let's think about it again regarding injury prevention.

In yoga practice, you'll commonly take a pose on one side of your body, and follow with the same on the other. Forward postures are balanced with backward, bends with stretches, and so on so that no one part of your body is overexerted.

Similarly, when you schedule your tasks, balance heavy and light, sitting and standing, and so on.

Take account of the weather and plan your physically demanding activities for cooler periods of the day, and lightest or rest periods during the hottest.

When you're ill, reduce your responsibilities and increase your rest breaks as much as possible.

While we're on the subject of self-care scheduling, make sure you schedule annual physical and six-monthly dental health check-ups too.

And just as you take leave from your paid work, plan to take a vacation from your housekeeping too. Now and again, get some help in, and if you can get away for a week to a health retreat, so much the better.

Physical Fitness

Even using wonderful time-saving appliances, cleaning is still a physical activity. Just like your spin class starts with a warm up to minimise your chances of injury, you could make some time to do some stretches before launching into your cleaning.

If you're managing long-term injuries such as tennis elbow or runner's knee apply the same taping or strapping you need for sustained physical activity. And when you're finished, do some cool down stretches (just like spin class).

If you've been unable to complete your housekeeping for a period of time, allow yourself time to rebuild your strength and stamina before going all in. Take your doctor's advice on how much activity to do.

Start with lighter duties and gradually build up. Don't over exert yourself as you may set your recovery back. Consider using a service until you're fully recovered.

In the 1950s, housewives were advised to change and put on makeup to look pretty for their tired homecoming husbands. It seems ludicrous today, but maybe it was more about her than him; a cue to let go of the concerns of her day and focus on enjoying grown-up time with her husband.

So, when you've finished your housekeeping, bathe and change just like a spin class. Mark the end of the housekeeping portion of your day and the start of your "real" work day.

Elizabeth Gilbert, author of *Big Magic: Creative Living Beyond Fear*, explains that when she finds herself suffering from writer's block, she "courts" her muse by bathing, shaving, doing her makeup and hair, and putting on some pretty clothes. If it works for her, I'm sure it can work for the rest of us.

Personal Protective Equipment

Think about extra layers of protection you need. Like gloves:

- "Rubber" for wet tasks like dishes and toilet cleaning.
- Cotton for sweeping, dusting and mopping.

- Thick for heavy physical tasks like storm recovery.

Don't forget items like aprons, head coverings, face masks, and closed shoes depending on what you're doing.

Housekeeping Outfit

In fact, you could even develop your own housekeeping uniform - you probably have exercise clothes, so why not?

I think most people feel better and achieve more when they feel well dressed than when they wear old rags that make them look and feel like a household slave.

You'll spend a lot of time taking care of your home, so why not make your outfit pretty as well as practical.

A practical housekeeping outfit will be loose enough to provide the most freedom of movement to waist and arms for bending, reaching, lifting, carrying and so on.

It should be made of a sufficiently durable material to offer you some protection from chemical spills, falling objects and getting caught on things.

Plus, you can do what hotels do and add an apron and cap to keep your hair neat and clean (or a ponytail and wash).

Consider whether you need pockets to store bits and bobs as you move through the house, or whether they'll be more of a hazard in your home.

To go with it, a low, closed toe, broad heeled shoe with a non-slip sole to support your spine and help prevent fallen arches. Maybe even your sneakers.

Use the Right Tools

Consider the ergonomics of your tasks, and think about the tools you could buy to help maintain a healthy posture.

For example, it's better to stand than stoop, so use long-handled tools, and bend from the waist. A good upright posture allows you to take deep breaths, ensures your organs are unrestricted and frees up blood circulation which keeps you mentally alert, as well as your feet and hands warm.

Buy tools and appliances that save you effort rather than creating more. Tools should be correctly scaled for your size, with grips designed to lessen the muscular strain.

As you move around the house completing your tasks, try to balance your load between your hands.

Set the Right Environment

Moving air is generally fresher than still as it contains fewer contaminants, so make sure your windows are open when you're using cleaning chemicals. If you can't open a window, only use chemicals in areas like bathrooms and kitchens where there's an extraction fan.

Mental Health

Health and safety is not just a physical concern, there's a mental component too.

Housekeeping can be stressful, partly because you're isolated, and partly because you're bombarded by advertising and social media suggesting you're not putting in enough effort (the morality thing) and are therefore a crap wife/mother.

Especially if you want a fulfilling life that doesn't revolve around your children. Or, you're a terrible wife/employee because you do.

It's best if you can maintain a sense of proportion.

Staying in Control

The physical labour is a significant part of housekeeping, and it helps to feel like you control it, not the other way around.

Not that you can actually control it, but feeling like you've a choice makes an enormous difference.

But you can't like you've a say when you feel like you're its slave. You won't feel in control if you believe:

- Cleaning is an inescapable monster.
- Housekeeping is the same as homemaking.
- It has to be done again and again, not just once.
- You're inadequate, can't do it correctly, or can't get started let alone finish.

All of these beliefs sap your joy and morale. Better housekeeping beliefs are:

- The world won't end if it's not done today.
- Housekeeping is a means to an end, not an end in itself.
- It's not the worse thing you'll ever have to do.
- You can be as innovative and creative as if you were working anywhere else.

Housekeeping does not involve moral judgements. It is what it is, there is no good/bad or right/wrong about it.

Learning to control your attention helps you see through household chaos and focus on the matters at hand. You don't need to spend all your time in a panic about keeping up.

In fact, that can decrease your efficiency. Sorry to be a bit 1950s (again), but developing poise will help you ignore the anxiety about not being enough, and master your to-do list.

Not just the housekeeping, but all of it. You'll be better able to deal with the feeling that housekeeping is a trap you've fallen into, or traditional drudgery, or the search for perfection, or more important than your other work and interests.

There is *nothing* wrong with you if you don't make it more important than everything else.

You need to develop a calm, rational mind so you can dispassionately examine household problems and assess possible solutions before deciding the best course of action. You need to learn to see things as they are, and be interested enough to increase your efficiency and productivity where you can in managing and organising your home.

And just as learning to meditate helps to calm stressed out executives, it can help you too. But you're luckier than them, you can lie down and rest or meditate for 10 - 20 minutes at any time that suits your needs. Maybe that's a mid-morning nap when the baby goes down. Or perhaps mid-afternoon before the evening business of cooking, picking up kids from school and so on gets started. It's up to you.

Summary

- Housekeeping is simply managing household affairs.
- In the paid workforce, each role is performed by a different person.
- You deserve the same level of respect and concern as the professional.
- Taking care of your physical and mental wellbeing is part of managing household affairs.
- You do not have to do it all yourself.

CHAPTER 2

Why Do Housekeeping?

WHEN YOU WERE VERY YOUNG, you wanted to know everything.

- Why is the sky blue?
- Why does that lady's face look funny?
- Why can't I sing that song?

Why, why, why you demanded, until your parents threatened you with grievous bodily harm. And probably a bit more after that until they shouted at or maybe smacked you.

Annoying as you were, you needed to know the answers because they helped you understand the universe and your place in it. You learned how to behave appropriately and safely around other people.

As time passed, you started experimenting on your own. You learned not to touch red (hot) things because it hurt when you did. You learned not to poke ants with sticks because they ran up the stick and bit you.

And when you brought flowers in from the garden, you were rewarded with hugs.

Every action you took brought some kind of result, and you used those results to figure out how to be safe in the world.

Later still, you came to understand that eating food that smelled a bit funny made you ill, that when you visited your friend with chicken pox, you caught it too, and if you didn't take care of your cuts they didn't heal well. You learned that you needed to wash your hands a lot so that you didn't get sick.

And when it comes to housekeeping, there are a few whys as well; though you get to choose those yourself.

Your Vision

I think the most influential housekeeping Why is your vision of your ideal future. You're probably not intending to live in a cardboard box under a bridge, but without a conscious effort to avoid that future, you could end up there.

It's more likely you imagine living in a clean and comfortable home, married to someone wonderful with a couple of angelic kids or pets who adore you. There's probably fresh air, good health, and a great deal of sunshine and happiness.

Bringing visions to fruition starts with setting goals and trying to achieve them - the clearer your vision is, the more likely you are to get there. You can focus on living in a clean and comfortable home every day, but someone wonderful and kids might take a little longer.

Your Home's Purpose

On a related note, your home's purpose provides another housekeeping Why.

In days gone by that might have been security, requiring a castle (with moat and drawbridge). Or perhaps home was a factory producing food, clothes and the other necessities of life. Or a battery farm producing the next generation of labourers to power the nation.

These days you probably have a different idea, though it may seem as esoteric to others:

- A soothing sanctuary from the hustle and bustle of life.

- An educational establishment for learning exciting new facts.

- Vegan Vittles test kitchen.

These are just three that I've heard, though of course, people didn't actually describe them that way.

If you take a moment to imagine what those places look like, you might come up with something like a:

- Clean, calm and uncluttered house, with white or pale pastel walls. The rooms are scented by fresh flowers and net curtains wave in the breeze from the open window. You can hear the tinkle of a water feature from the garden.

- A dimly lit library with dust motes floating in the sunlight. There are red leather Chesterfields, wood occasional tables, floor to ceiling shelves stuffed with books, magazines and papers. In fact, probably all the flat surfaces are covered with stacks of books, magazines and papers. (Ah bliss...)

- Stainless steel kitchen counters and appliances. White subway tiles on the wall and an easy-clean linoleum on the floor. A massive pantry full of fresh produce, herbs and spices, and mysterious packets of exotic ingredients. Open shelves with assorted cookware stacked in easy reach.

And as you can probably guess, each of these homes requires different levels of care and attention.

- Daily tidying up and putting away, changing the flower water and throwing out the dead/dying blooms. Regular vacuuming, dusting and curtain washing.

- Removing used crockery and cutlery daily. Now and again conditioning the leather seating, rearranging the stacks for ease of passage, and filing the papers. Shutting the door so no one can get in there and mess it up (because you know exactly where everything is).

- Cleaning (maybe scrubbing) floors, walls and surfaces at least once daily. Frequent stock takes and shopping trips to replenish supplies. Having the plumber, electrical and dishwasher service company on speed dial.

In general, we don't tend to consider the implications of some of our choices on other aspects of our lives, so if you want to minimise your housekeeping commitment, you may need to reconsider your home's purpose as well.

Your Purpose

Some people have steadfast opinions that their purpose in life is to create an immaculate home. That's fine, but if that's your purpose, then you might as well put this book down now because that purpose doesn't leave any space for anything other than continuous ongoing cleaning and tidying until you die. Not spending time with your partner, or your children, or even flicking through a magazine.

But if your purpose is to inspire and motivate your children, you need to make the time and space to develop that.

You can only use each hour once, so you've choices to make about what tasks you undertake as well as how much time you give to them each day.

For example, you might want a clean and uncluttered home because you need a feeling of lightness to inspire yourself before you can inspire others.

So, you decorate your home with built-in cupboards, streamlined furniture and a minimalist design aesthetic. You choose to vacuum every morning and imagine you're vacuuming up distractions that could take you away from your work.

At the end of the day, you put everything away so you can spend your evenings with the people and activities that nurture your soul. And when you start in the morning, you see an expanse of emptiness waiting to be filled.

Your Health

Your future vision of good health in part relies on good housekeeping to eliminate or minimise the risks of tiny invisible things like germs, gas leaks, and allergens that can make you or your family ill.

You're managing indoor air quality by:

- Choosing building products and finishes that don't off-gas pollutants like volatile organic compounds or formaldehyde that irritate eyes, nose and throats.

- Not allowing people to smoke indoors.

- Vacuuming up dust mites and allergens to minimise eczema, asthma, and other respiratory issues.

- Cleaning bathrooms to minimise mould spores that aggravate asthma, and lead to nasal irritations.

- Opening windows to allow fumes like carbon monoxide and nitrogen dioxide (that can kill in sufficient concentration) to escape.

You're also making strategic decisions about furnishings:

- Household plants to improve air quality.

- Easy to clean furnishings and fabrics.

- Low emission, easy to clean floor and wall coverings.

- Wood, gas, or electric heating with adequate air filtration and external venting.

And what you do inside it:

- Are shoes on or off.
- Are pets in or out?
- The types of air fresheners and cleaning products you use.

Your Abilities

It might be that your physical or mental capacities, dexterity, stamina and ability limit what you can reasonably achieve.

For the sake of your self-esteem, it's important to be honest with yourself about what you can do, and what you need help with. Life is stressful enough without believing you can't even keep up with the cleaning as well.

For example, temporary or permanent sports injuries, as well as being painful, can limit your physical ability to bend, reach, or grasp in the course of completing your tasks. They can also impede your mobility, or your ability to sit or stand for long enough to get them done.

Your Safety

The main reason we live in buildings is that they offer a level of protection from the weather, enemy armies, and man-eating predators. You can be reasonably secure in the knowledge that when you go to sleep, you will wake up in the morning. Those things are more or less taken care of when you shut the door.

But if you don't take care of your home, you can create other risks that threaten your safety; obstacles to trip over, objects that fall on you (or you fall off), or that can choke/suffocate you. Sometimes small poisonous creatures like snakes and spiders depending on where you live.

You can use the same regular habits and long-term risk management systems to care for yourself and manage household risks. For example, minimising your risk of carbon monoxide poisoning by servicing your gas appliances, installing detectors, and keeping your house well ventilated.

Exercise

My usual approach to cleaning is to get it over and done with as quickly as possible.

At least it was until I got an activity tracker and started getting serious about improving my health. I wouldn't say I welcome or seek out the opportunity to trot backwards and forwards throughout the house picking things up and putting them away, but it might be a more useful way to add a few hundred purposeful steps than doing laps of the garden.

Plus, you can burn off a couple of hundred calories by pursuing your cleaning with vigorous intention, as opposed to listless, half-hearted, dragging your feet to get the job done. Particularly more physical tasks like making beds, moving furniture (to clean underneath it), and scrubbing bathtubs. And if you have a garden, getting out there and weeding, raking, or pushing a lawnmower.

Not only that, an activity like mopping floors will help with flexibility, balance, and strength. And washing windows (by hand with a spray) does the same.

You could also include specific muscle building exercises in your cleaning routine, such as lunging while you vacuum and squatting or doing leg lifts instead of bending. Doing it faster burns even more calories too! Just Google "housework workout" for more ideas.

If exercise is one of your reasons, you may need to allow more time to get it done, because washing dishes by hand can take a lot longer than stacking the dishwasher. Or you could challenge yourself to get more repetitions in less time, but be mindful of your safety while you're doing the exercises.

You could also take a brisk walk around the block to develop your fitness, stamina and resilience at the of your "work out" before you shower and move on with the rest of your day.

Other People's Expectations

In the early days of writing this book, I ran a little survey to find out what people thought about housework (see Appendix B: Housework Survey Says: What You Really Think About It for the results).

I was interested to find that far and away the biggest housekeeping motivator is fear of what other people think. Peace of mind came second, but only very slightly more important than concern about rodents, bugs, germs and the like.

I suppose it's not really that surprising when we can't help but judge others by the condition of their clothes, cars, and houses. When we see people who don't look neat and clean, we assume they are somehow less capable than "normal" people who present themselves in a way more acceptable to us.

When we see cars full of old takeout containers and empty drink bottles, we might think the owner is shiftless or homeless because they can't even put their rubbish in the bin.

Similarly, when we visit people's homes, and they are littered with papers, stacks of books or magazines, and other personal items, we can't help but wonder if it's safe to sit down.

And if the sink is full of unwashed dishes, and the bin needs emptying, we might worry that the place is unhygienic and refuse a drink in case we get ill. We might even cut our visit short and leave quickly.

To an extent, you have to think of your future self as a judgey person too. One day, you'll decide to sort out old photos, and as well as wondering where you were and how you knew those people, you'll probably be a little shocked at how messy your house was.

And a little embarrassed that you were socialising next to a basket of laundry, a stack of dirty dishes, or a bowl full of rotting fruit. And you might realise that if you throw out all those photos, you won't have any left...

Don't be disheartened, it's not your fault. It's just that you didn't learn how to take care of all this.

You might have been told to clean your room, but not what cleaning was - I'm fairly sure I'm not the only person on the planet who thought that shoving everything under my bed or in the wardrobe was all that was required.

You didn't learn the Why of cleaning your room, and if your mother was like mine, you never needed to because sooner or later, she caved and did it for you.

And so, your home has become an extension of your bedroom, except your mother doesn't clean it for you anymore, so it doesn't get done. You don't put anything away, or in the bin - it's all out there for all to see. And you're so used to the stacks of stuff, and drifts of detritus that you just don't see it anymore.

It's not the nicest motivator, but if all else fails, invite someone round to eat and get it done.

Summary

- Work to achieve your vision of the future.
- Understand your home's purpose.
- Discovering your Why may be the most critical housekeeping task you complete.
- Staying healthy is a pretty good motivator.
- If all else fails, invite someone for dinner.

CHAPTER 3

Who Does the Housekeeping?

WHEN YOU GET DOWN TO it, robotics has not progressed far enough to take care of everything that needs to be done.

You can get a cute little robotic vacuum cleaner, but you still need to empty it (every five minutes). You've an automatic clothes washer, but you still need to put the clothes in and pull them out when they're done.

Even with a combined washer and dryer, you need to empty it between washing and drying or you end up with a lump of laundry that's dry on the outside and wet on the inside.

You still need people for housekeeping.

You

Clearly, you're doing the bulk of it otherwise you wouldn't be reading this book.

And to be blunt, if you are doing it, the rest of your household literally could not care less about it. They probably aren't doing anything whatsoever to assist you, showing a complete disregard for the value of your time.

If they are disregarding (or disrespecting you), consider whether you could be the stumbling block on the path to an efficient household.

Have you ever re-stacked the dishwasher after your partner filled it up because it wasn't "right"? Or refolded the laundry because your kids can't fold in neat squares?

Then you're not only getting in your own way but creating unnecessary effort for yourself and potentially damaging your relationships as well.

Could you take a step back and care less too?

You may feel that it's your job to take care of the big and small people who share your home, and you're probably right about that, but there's taking care of and taking care of. Just like there's a difference between satisfying their needs and wants. And balancing their wants with your needs.

You may not want to cede control of some tasks because you don't believe that your partner or children can do them as well or as quickly as you. And you're probably right about that too. At least for the first few times, but there is very little that can go earth-shatteringly wrong in the housekeeping arena, and what does can generally be easily rectified.

Just like in business, delegating tasks to other people frees up your time for other activities. If you can make each resident responsible for their room, that's fewer rooms for you to take care of, and less time you need to spend on them.

Another thing to consider, is that now and again your other "jobs" will demand more of your time, and as we've already discussed, there are only 24 hours available to you; every minute is a choice between one task or another.

When you have to "do an all-nighter", regardless of whether that's in your business, your paid work, or taking care of sick pets or relatives, that time has to come from one of your other jobs. And that's often your housekeeping anyway.

On the other hand, there may be logical and sensible reasons why you're doing it all. If you're not happy about it, and can't get help from elsewhere, then you've two options: do it with a good will, or do it with a bad will.

Jennifer L. Scott, author of *At Home with Madame Chic: Becoming a connoisseur of daily life*, suggests that it's possible to imbue your housekeeping with a sense of devotion or divine purpose because your home is the place from which all your other activities start.

In fact, the love and attention you give your personal appearance can be extended to your home. In a sense, your home is your most intimate garment you wear all the time. And just as you should lavish love and attention on your body, so you should on your home, because it protects and cherishes you.

Your Partner

I'm just going to say it - you're sharing a house so you can share the housekeeping. In fact, the likelihood is that you already do. You may have the inside work, and your partner the outside. Or maybe you cook, and they do the dishes. Or some other kind of arrangement that you've fallen into.

This may be a contentious area, and will probably involve some difficult conversations, but it's mainly about setting expectations. I don't think it's unreasonable to expect your partner to make the same basic level of effort you expect of your kids. For example, putting their washing in the laundry hamper, hanging up their towels, and putting their dirty dishes in the dishwasher.

These are tiny tasks that only take a couple of minutes per person, but if you do it all, eat up ten minutes of your time. And you could get a lot done if you spent that ten minutes on your other activities - the ones you think are more important than housekeeping.

Jennifer Granger, author of *Feminine Lost: Why Most Women are Male,* argues that all people are a dynamic balance of masculine (yang) and feminine (yin) energy.

In its essence, masculine energy is active; doing and giving. And as you'd expect, feminine energy is creative; it nurtures and receives. You choose from your feminine aspect but act from your masculine.

When you get two people in a room, regardless of their gender or sexuality, they will tend to balance each other out. You might have noticed this as a child, knowing which parent to approach for what favour.

Minimally Viable Housekeeping

So far so good, but when you're too doing in your approach, you tip your partner into receiving. Why would they do anything when you're already doing it? If you step back a bit, they have the opportunity to give, and you to receive.

Of course, you'll have to negotiate the transfer of tasks, but you don't both have to lose, you can both win in the exchange. You can negotiate an outcome that works for both of you, though you'll need to allow time for them to catch up with you.

You're probably juggling a lot, so let me stay contentious and ask what your partner is juggling. Are they contributing in proportion to your sacrifices?

And if you were to fall ill with the flu (or worse), would you still be juggling or would your partner be attempting to catch some of the balls? And is it really necessary that all those balls be in the air anyway?

I don't mean to imply that your partner is the crux of the problem; while a world of opportunity has opened for women, men are still bound by the expectations of days gone by.

We can't ask for equal pay, but they can't ask for time off, and in some cases are more alienated from family life than they would like. (Though I know that not all partners are male).

For minimally viable housekeeping to function on an ongoing basis, you may need to lower your standards. It doesn't matter how the laundry gets in the hamper, because you're going to sort it anyway.

Nor does it matter how the towels look when they are hung up, or how the dishes get stacked in the dishwasher.

If you continually tell the love of your life what and how to do things, they (like you) will resist that instruction. And if you rearrange the dishwasher every time they put something in it, they will stop doing it.

There is a point where instructing others how to do tasks to your satisfaction slides into nagging. It is the naggee that decides when that line has been crossed, not the nagger, and this causes the tension in a relationship. Not to mention that some naggees will seek out more pleasant people to be with.

In paid work, time and quality pressures from your boss and customers, often mean you settle for good enough (as opposed to perfect) so why should you aim higher when you're working for free? Learn to live with good enough.

And while I think about it, Annabelle Crabb reminds us in her book *The Wife Drought: Why women need wives, and men need lives*, that sometimes our partners will make us gifts of housework, quite separate from their usual tasks.

I think these mustn't be taken for granted, they must always be acknowledged as the special love tokens they are. Particularly if you'd like more of them.

For that matter, why not thank your partner for doing their usual chores as well - we all like our efforts acknowledged.

Your Kids

I know there are a lot of parents who think it's important their children do their homework and study hard, so they get into good universities, earn advantageous qualifications, get steady jobs with high incomes and live successful lives. (And can, therefore, afford to put them into decent nursing homes).

Giving them chores helps develop their physical and mental skills, and prepares them to move out on their own. It also gives a sense of ownership and pride in their home and family.

Of course, you need to give them defined tasks and a "wage" so they can learn to manage their money. Make sure that cleaning up after themselves is on the list!

Then you can let them move out of home, confident in the knowledge you've taught them to function as adults. They can cook well enough to sustain themselves, they know how to use a clothes washer, balance their credit card statement and create a clean and inviting living space.

If only so when you visit them, you spend a pleasant couple of hours catching up with their news, not cleaning their home or sitting gingerly on the edge of your seat trying not to touch anything. And when they come home to visit, they might not bring their laundry with them.

Naturally, younger children are less capable than older, but more likely to want to do things for and with their parents so the sooner you get onto this, the better your results will be!

You can start by helping them to pull up the comforter on their bed (you'll be doing it either way), but at some point, they will be able to do it themselves.

Potentially, by the time you reach the Age of Rebellion, their housekeeping habits are so ingrained they will do their chores without your nagging.

Where it gets tricky is the kind of school project (like taking care of a class pet or mascot) that's technically the child's responsibility, but everyone knows Mum does it.

Your Pets

Pets can be taught an amazing array of tricks if you've the patience and a good stack of treats.

As well as playing dead, dogs can be taught to put their toys away, defecate in particular areas of the garden (or the toilet), fetch their leads and food bowls (or your slippers), pick up and dispose of rubbish (e.g., tissues and sweet wrappers).

Despite conventional wisdom, cats can be trained to do dog tricks too, including defecating in particular places (litter boxes or toilets), walk on a lead, fetch, and put their toys away.

Much better trick than shaking hands don't you think?

Outsourcing

Often, when a business wants to save money, it will sack some staff and hire a firm to perform those tasks or produce those goods. Particularly in areas like recruitment and call centres.

You're probably more interested in saving time than money, but the principle's the same; you're paying someone else to do the work.

In the old days, you had no choice but to hire someone local, now you can go online and get stuff done on the other side of the planet while you sleep.

There are two main ways to do it:

- **Virtual services:** these are usually at the administration end of the housekeeping spectrum; planning, scheduling, dispatching, researching, purchasing and accounting. They are generally performed or delivered online by programs, applications, or people you never meet.

- **In-person services:** these are the physical housekeeping tasks; cooking, cleaning, laundry, caring and property management. While you may organise these online, they involve people coming to your home.

The idea of someone else taking care of the tasks you can't is very tempting, and if you can afford it, an excellent solution. But it comes with some caveats.

- You're trusting your private information (e.g., name, address, credit card and other identifiable information) to someone else. You need to be very sure that they will secure it adequately, and notify you immediately they discover their security has been breached so you can act to protect your information security.

- You're letting a stranger into your home; they have access to all your belongings and computers as well as your children and pets. You'd be wise to hire through an agency that performs police checks, ensures candidates have impeccable references, and guarantees a high level of performance. You also need to decide if you want the same person every time, or just the same tasks completed, and it doesn't matter who does them.

- You need to provide precise instructions about what you want them to do and the quality of the end result. If they don't meet your expectations, you need to give feedback on what they must do better. Plus, you need to consider what action you will take should items get broken or go missing. And at some point, you may need to dismiss them and find someone new to take over.

- You've the responsibility of paying for satisfactory work, and if the work isn't, negotiating its remediation.

In-Person Services

Services performed by people come in several types.

Live In

Live in help, comes in different forms:

- *Au pairs*: young people from foreign countries who work part-time cleaning and caring for children in return for an allowance. Some also study English.

- A housekeeper à la Mrs Hughes who does everything while you get on with your paid work.

- A maid who cleans, and maybe cooks too.

- A nanny to take care of your children.
- A nurse/carer to take care of people who are ill or have special needs.

Live in staff often have salary packages that include board and food as well as wages and other benefits such as vacations, retirement savings, and access to a car for personal use.

The likelihood is that you'll hire through an agency who will help you negotiate that, but you'll probably be the direct employer with all the legal obligations that go along with that.

Paid staff need a job description representing an agreement between you that they will meet your expectations on tasks, responsibilities and knowledge, and you will meet their expectations on wages, hours of work, and breaks.

For example, one basic expectation to meet is a private room at their disposal - one you don't enter except by invitation. Another is set hours of work, though you might also include a process for negotiating extra hours or duties, and incentives like extra pay or time off.

And if you'd like that person there for the long-term, you'll need to think about performance reviews and management, as well as higher pay for higher productivity or skills acquisition.

Downton Abbey servants were more a part of the family than is usual today, but people who feel their interests are served by their employers are generally more supportive and flexible in their approach to their work.

Live Out

If you're not fond of the idea of a stranger living in your home, you can hire the same types of roles to come in. That might be one person full-time 40 hours a week, or one or more people a few hours a day or week, or for ad hoc projects like Spring cleaning or after storm garden clean ups.

You could become the direct employer, or hire an agency that sends someone in to take care of the tasks you need to be done although this may not be the same person every time.

Functional

These are businesses you hire for specific assistance, such as pre-prepared meals, dog walking or shopping. Some operate on a subscription model where you pay per month regardless of the level of service you use, others on a pay per use basis.

Professional

Professional services are specialised functional services including accounting, legal and medical services. They're usually paid by the job (e.g., to prepare your will) or by the hour.

Summary

- If you're taking care of everything, no one else could care less.
- Changing the way you look at your home can change the way you feel about taking care of it.
- Try to keep your relationships in balance.
- Partners, children and pets can take responsibility for their rooms and make other minimal contributions.
- If you can afford it, there are services to help with tasks you don't like or find difficult.

CHAPTER 4

When Does It Get Done?

IF YOU'VE BEEN COPING ON an ad hoc basis, it's only fair to warn your household they'll be moving to a schedule.

For example, they need to know which days are laundry days so they can make sure that their clothes are ready to wash. Initially, you'll need to remind them it's laundry day and if it's not in the hamper it won't get washed, but over time they'll adjust. You can make up your own mind about exceptions to your "if it's not there it won't get washed" rule.

There'll be resistance, but remember you're transitioning to a schedule for minimally viable housekeeping. You've other, potentially more important things to do, and are minimising your housekeeping commitments to focus on them.

When you complete these tasks and projects takes us back to your Why and Who. When you understand them, you can pull it into a 12-month calendar that fits your unique circumstances and allows you to ensure everything gets done.

But before we do that, let's think about an Ideal Day.

Your Ideal Day

In his book, *The Time Trap: The Classic Book on Time Management,* Alec Mackenzie introduces the concept of an "Ideal Day." It's the perfect day that takes advantage of your natural high and low energy periods, includes time for uninterrupted work, and all your tasks are completed quickly and easily.

At the end of it, you're closer to achieving your goals, with sufficient energy left to enjoy some high-quality leisure time.

If you're not sure when the right time for that uninterrupted work is, Dank Pink is here to help out. In his book *When: The Scientific Secrets of Perfect Timing* he tells us that in general, our mood rises in the morning, dips in the afternoon and rises again in the evening.

The exact timing depends on what your chronotype is - morning people are at their peak in the morning, and unsurprisingly, night owls are at theirs at night. Interestingly, trying to work outside your hours can be as hard as trying to work at the legal alcohol limit!

However, in general, it's best to do analytic work in your chronotype's "morning" when you're fresh, and your creative work in the chronotype afternoon. Or the important stuff at your peak, and the second most important in your recovery.

And when I say your important stuff, I mean do the work you get paid for at your peak, and the work you don't get paid for in the slump.

The Ideal Day is, of course, unachievable, but as it's a broad outline of the kind of day where everything goes right, and you get everything done that you need to, it makes a good basic template for planning out your tasks.

Example Ideal Day

The first thing to note is that an ideal day has a start and a finish - you clock on, and you clock off. For the purpose of this example, we'll start with the time you get up and the time you go to bed, say 6 am to 10 pm.

If you've got a paying job, say 9 am to 2 pm, then you'll block those hours (plus your commute) off your schedule because you'll be using different methods to manage that time. This leaves you with two time slots to get stuff done; 6 am to 8 am, and 3 pm to 10 pm.

Most probably, your morning slot will be taken up by preparing breakfasts and lunches, getting kids and partners off to work, and getting yourself ready and off to work.

You could block this time off for that purpose, but it might be that you can create habits to make good use of the available time in the place you're located. For example, emptying the dishwasher while you make coffee, doing a quick load of laundry, or starting to prepare dinner.

You can also start creating helpful habits in the rest of the family; putting their dishes in the washer, making their beds, hanging up their towels.

That leaves you with the 3 pm to 10 pm after work slot.

Even Mrs Hughes clocked off when the day was done, so I'm telling you to set a time that marks the end of your working day. Let's say 6 pm in this scenario - this marks your transition to Lady Cora. No household tasks, just time spent enjoying your family.

So, the bulk of your housekeeping time is going to be 3 pm to 6 pm. Three hours a day seems (and is) a lot of time for that, but during that time you'll be doing your daily, weekly and scheduled tasks as well as whatever needs to be done to give you those few "responsibility free" hours to enjoy, just like everyone else in the house.

Ms Blaelock's Ideal Day

I've been using a version of an ideal day since 1997 when I bought Mackenzie's book hoping it could help me manage the competing demands of working for several bosses. I do find it a useful way to prioritise the big picture of my day.

At the moment, my ideal day looks like this:

- 6:15 am Get out of bed and make coffee. Let the dogs out, set off the clothes washer, empty the dishwasher. Soak up some quiet time with DB.

- 7:00 Make and eat breakfast.

- 7:30 Clear up breakfast, make lunch, feed dogs and start my regular scheduled housekeeping (e.g., laundry, administration, cleaning toilets, etc.).

- 8:30 Finish housekeeping, take a walk, bathe, dress.

Minimally Viable Housekeeping

9:00	Paid editing and writing.
1:00 pm	Lunch, misc
2:00	My writing.
5:00	Finish work, feed the dogs and start dinner.
5:30	Clear my desk, update my time sheets and progress notes, start a to-do list for tomorrow.
6:00	Finish dinner and leftover housekeeping.
6:30	Eat, tidy up, stack dishwasher.
7:00	Watch tv, enjoy quality time with DB and dogs.
10:30	Quick kitchen tidy, run dishwasher, clean teeth and face and go to bed.

Remember, it's my ideal day - it doesn't always go to plan.

Even when I swap bits of my day around, I tend to get my best work done in the afternoon. So, I try to get the bulk of my housekeeping out of the way early so I can focus on my paid work. Where possible, I make my services, deliveries and external appointments early in the morning for the same reason.

I live out of town, so if I have an appointment, I almost always end up losing an entire working day. I try to double up my housekeeping on adjacent days, but it's not going to matter much if a task doesn't get done one week.

On those days, I allow myself a guilt-free housekeeping-free day, but try to schedule as many appointments as I can, including lunch or coffee with friends!

And remembering that it's an ideal day, if I'm sleepy, I might take a nap after lunch, or move my walk instead. Sometimes I'll start work earlier, work later, or take a longer lunch to do the housework.

Planning Your Daily Schedule

I've given you a couple of examples, but of course, yours will be different. No two homes are the same; they contain different numbers of people (and animals), have different locations, are constructed of different materials, and have different routines. Your schedule is what makes the sheer variety of tasks achievable within the time allowed.

Having said that, most homes will at least require daily meal preparation and clean up, bed making and perhaps light cleaning or tidying the house.

You might start by following Mrs Patmore's lead and schedule around fixed and immovable meal times. Decide whether to clean up breakfast before you do the bedrooms or when you prepare lunch. Will you go straight from the bedrooms to the light cleaning, or would it be better to get the dinner on and give the house a quick once over before everyone gets home?

Some families need flexible schedules that take account of their particular circumstances:

- Infants; for example, nap times.

- Elderly; such as allowing extra time to help them complete activities.

- Illness; for example, medication schedules.

- Shift Workers; embargoing some times of the day so they can get some sleep.

- Animals or Livestock; such as feeding.

You can also chunk tasks that happen in the same place, for example, preparing the vegetables for dinner, washing the lunch dishes and cooking dessert to free up more free time later in the day. Or reviewing the refrigerator and pantry contents after breakfast so the meals can be planned and a shopping list written.

Just remember that your schedule is just a way for you to get things done. It's not a thing that needs to be done; basing it on your Ideal Day helps you make it fit your circumstances, not the other way around.

Planning Your Weekly Schedule

You probably already have some kind of regular schedule tied to external drivers such as your rubbish collection, and the different types of activity and leisure schedules your family keeps (e.g. Tuesday afternoon football practice or Thursday morning Skype calls to the office).

These commitments slot into your daily schedule, and you layer other tasks around them.

Now and again, you'll have to take part or all of a day off from housekeeping to attend external appointments or do bigger jobs like storm clean up, painting, or window washing.

On those days, try not to stress too much about your schedule. Check to see what else is on, and consider whether you can reschedule tasks, or skip them until next week. Try not to reschedule them too often!

You might also like to think of the seasonality of your housekeeping. Some days you can dry your laundry outside, others you'll use the dryer. Is there a best day to do your washing? Should you do your fridge and pantry cleaning the day before your rubbish is collected? How often you need/want to dust, clean your oven, and wash your bathtub?

Planning Your Monthly Schedule

You may also have some form of monthly schedule - many activities such as farmers markets and professional development happen on a rotating monthly calendar, (e.g., the second Tuesday or third Sunday).

Even if you don't, you might like to use a monthly schedule for planning a lighter/deeper cleaning schedule. For example, you might dust daily, wipe greasy weekend fingerprints off the furniture on Mondays, and on the last Monday of each month, lovingly polish your wood furniture with beeswax.

Planning Your Quarterly Schedule

Similarly, you may have a quarterly schedule, probably in the form of seasonal preparations such as preparing for the Summer bushfire or Winter storm seasons. Or your Spring and Autumn wardrobe swaps,

Planning Your Annual Schedule

You also have an annual plan, which is most recognisable in birthdays, religious observances and sales shopping.

It's useful to start adding in tasks like servicing your climate control, replacing small appliances and testing the market to see if your insurances (etc.) are still the best ones for you.

Some people find it easier to start with an annual plan of all the tasks they'd like to complete each year, and then allocate them to seasons, then to months and the weeks.

This list would include all the things that you wouldn't usually think about doing, for example, cleaning doors and their handles, light switches, fans, climate control vents and fixtures, washing blankets, airing quilts, cleaning curtains, vacuuming couches, sweeping chimneys, washing windows, cleaning cupboard interiors and exteriors, clearing cobwebs, cleaning ovens and range hoods.

Not to mention inspecting your home's exterior roof, floor tiling, piping, driveways, gutters and so on for cleaning, maintain and repair.

And if you're a gardener, your key dates for planting, pruning, propagating, mulching, and spraying.

Planning Your Longer-Term Schedule

You might not know it, but you also have regular commitments that take place over a time-frame longer a year.

These activities are more like major projects, generally in the form of household maintenance like replacing furnaces and water heaters or repainting your window trims.

It can also include medical care like repeat tests and vaccinations, or replacement fillings and implants.

I am aware that it seems like overkill to plan an event that won't happen for a decade, but if you don't have some kind of bring forward system, it's likely it will be forgotten.

And that sounds as though it will probably be fine, but what if that event is replacing your water heater? You might find that when it breaks down, you don't have the funds to replace it. Or there might not be stock on hand so you may have to wait for several days for one to come in. Or installation may be delayed. Much better to have a note to remind yourself in nine and a half years to replace it before it breaks down.

Minor Tasks in the Schedule

Your schedule usually only includes the large jobs that occur regularly. But you know there are also little tasks, like putting your tools away or emptying the kitchen bin that happen frequently but not regularly.

You can add them to your standard procedures, for example emptying the bin at the conclusion of your meal clean up or tidy kitchen tasks.

Alternatively, you can habituate them, for example, put your tools away when you finish the job.

You can also plan activities to minimise future disruptions, for example, shopping to ensure that deliveries occur at regular, predictable times, and you've sufficient cash on hand to pay or tip for it as it arrives.

Major Tasks in the Schedule

At some point, you'll bring one of your long-term projects (e.g., repainting the house) into your short-term schedule. At those times consider taking a "vacation" from your regular housekeeping - there's not much point cleaning in the morning when it's going to look as though you haven't done anything by the end of the day anyway.

Actual Form of Schedule

Once you've developed your best schedule, make a permanent record of it. You could use a day to a page diary, a monthly calendar, or a tickler file system. Try it out for at least two weeks to see if it makes a difference and keep a notebook nearby so you can note any problems you're having and potential solutions.

Summary

- Use an "Ideal Day" for your planning framework.
- Plan around your existing commitments.
- Include short, medium, and long-term commitments.

CHAPTER 5

Where Does it all Happen?

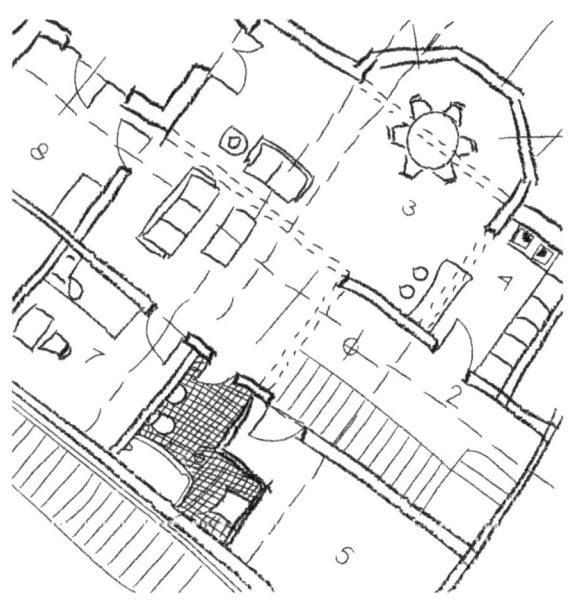

ONE OF THE MANY THINGS you don't see in *Downton Abbey* (or your hotel) is maids scuttling about after the family leaves a room to clean and reset it ready for their return. Nor do you see them doing their version of a daily and weekly clean. Maids work(ed) long days, and they were cleaning and tidying all day. That was their job.

You're not a maid. It's not your job, so you don't need (or probably want) to scamper around after the rest of the household all day and night. Think back to your Why for a moment - it ultimately governs your practices.

Before You Get Home

The primary way to ensure minimally viable housekeeping is to stop stuff getting through the front door!

This includes adopting a range of techniques to leave physical dirt and clutter outside:

- Using a range of products (e.g., doormats),
- Developing new habits (e.g., discarding junk mail before you enter the house),
- Refusing free giveaways that don't fulfil an identified need,
- Buying what you need and no more,
- Being incredibly picky about what you buy.

And depending on your vision, and home's purpose, you may need to develop some techniques for leaving mental dirt and clutter outside the door too.

Minimally Viable Housekeeping

Buying

Before you buy anything, ask yourself if it's really necessary, followed by whether you'll use it often enough to justify the maintenance cost - in time and money.

Tools need the correct care to remain efficient; can you (will you) care for it properly by oiling the machinery or sharpening the blades? Or using the right detergent? Allowing cookware to gradually come up to heat, not using it at too high, or submitting it to sudden changes in temperature?

If you can't or won't look after your purchases, reconsider whether you should be buying them.

At Home

Your home has zones with different traffic and use patterns that can guide the time and effort required to maintain them. If a room is rarely used, you don't need to give it as much attention as a room used daily by the whole family.

You may have some rooms that don't fit these categories, but the traffic v use formula will help you figure out what's required. My suggestions on the levels of care follow.

This is just somewhere to start. Just because I list it, doesn't mean I think you have to do it. Nor does it mean I think you have to do it all in the morning, though if you do it in the morning, it's done and you can forget about it until next time.

And it's not all-encompassing. If, for example, you have asthma sufferers you may need to do more cleaning more often. If you live in a tiny apartment or small studio with a wall/Murphy bed, you may not need to do as much because you don't have much space.

Public Rooms

These are the leisure/recreation rooms where you entertain guests. These probably require the highest levels of cleanliness and presentation - so much so that they might not be used by your family. In fact, the doors may be closed to them. As you don't use these rooms regularly, you're more likely to clean sporadically on demand.

Dining Room

If you have one, this is a formal room where you host dinner parties so it might not get much use. It may have higher quality furniture or fancy art that needs special care and is best separated from sticky young fingers.

My mother almost never used this room; the door was almost permanently closed and the furniture covered with drop sheets. When she entertained, she took the covers off and freshened the room. The bulk of the cleaning was after the dinner was over - the equivalent of maids or waitresses cleaning and resetting the room for the next sitting.

> **Daily:** Nothing
>
> **Weekly:** Nothing
>
> **Scheduled:** freshen before the event, clean and close down after the event.

Living/Sitting/Lounge Room

This room may be used more frequently, for coffee, card games, or other non-meal related entertainments. It's more likely to be used for spontaneous than planned events, so it's less formal and kept in a state of readiness.

It's also a room best cleaned on departure, which makes it the ideal room to practice bringing things out or putting them away when you're finished. Or not taking them in at all.

Daily: Remove dishes, rubbish and so on.

Weekly: Tidy, dust and vacuum.

Scheduled: Clean and close down after larger event such as a party.

Private Rooms

Private rooms are for family only, and you would only admit the closest of friends, so close they're almost family.

When you have guests, these are the rooms you're most likely to shut the doors to. Not because you're embarrassed about them, but because it's none of their business.

They'll be in constant use and require attention because they're high traffic areas, though the quality of cleanliness might not be as high as your public rooms.

Family Room

This is the room where your family spends most of its time hanging out together, watching television, playing games and so on. It may be mostly clean, but with all the comings and goings, keeping it tidy is another matter altogether. It's likely to be full of clutter and finding used dishes a treasure hunt.

Daily: Tidy, remove rubbish, perhaps vacuum.

Weekly: Dust and vacuum.

Scheduled: Seasonal tasks like carpet cleaning.

Bedrooms

Your bedroom is your most personal and intimate space. You sleep in this room and are therefore at your most defenceless in this space. And while it's my goal to die in my sleep, my preference would be peacefully, of old age. Not in a fire, suffocated by stacks of clutter, or poisoned by carbon monoxide.

I think making your children responsible for their own bedroom daily care is an excellent grounding for their future independence. Just remember to be very specific about your expectations.

Daily

- Open the windows to let in some fresh air. I leave mine open all the time, but it does mean more dusting.

- Throw/fold back the bed covers to air out the bed. A lot of people will advise you to make your bed first thing every day, so you start by having achieved something. But if you or your partner tend to sweat a lot, you might prefer to air it out instead. Don't just leave it as higgledy-piggledy as it was when you crawled out of it, fold your covers back neatly and air it as seriously others make their beds. This extra effort in the morning also makes it easier to quickly pull the covers up at bedtime.

- Tidy, remove rubbish, perhaps vacuum. (If you put away your clothes and shoes when you take them off, you'll have a nice uncluttered room to sleep in, and there's less to do in the morning).

- Make the bed (if you're a maker).

- Close the windows if you wish, and depending on the season, adjust the blinds/curtains to block the hot summer sun.

- If you like, shut the door to show it's done. Or leave it open for airflow.

Weekly: dust, vacuum, mop

Scheduled

- "Proper" dust with a damp cloth; surfaces and ornaments. Even better, wash them in warm soapy water or approved cleaner.

- Wash sheets. How often you wash them depends on how many people and pets sleep in and on the bed, whether they're naked or bathe before bed. Plus, whether they are there every night, are ill, or eat or drink in bed. The more of those you say yes to, the more often you should wash the sheets.

- Clean pillows, mattress toppers, bed skirts, bedspreads and so on as they're full of drool.

- Vacuum and rotate the mattress to clean and promote even wear.

Children's Play Rooms or Studies

Some families have a communal room the children share for TV, games, homework, or other activities. You could treat it as an adult-free zone and just shut the door, but I imagine you would prefer to check in now and again just to track down all those glasses and cups that go missing.

It's up to you to decide how much you'll make them responsible for, even if that's just putting things away so you can duck in and vacuum.

Daily: Tidy, remove rubbish, perhaps vacuum.

Weekly: Dust and vacuum.

Scheduled: Seasonal tasks like carpet cleaning.

Functional Rooms

Functional rooms are those like kitchens, laundries or home offices where you fulfil particular functions.

You might, in some circumstances let guests in, but because there they're task-oriented areas, you may have activities in progress that you don't want disturbed. Each has a different level of cleanliness partly based on use (e.g., food hygiene v client meetings) and partly on the level of traffic they receive.

Kitchen

Given its role in nourishing your family, this is one of the most important rooms in your home, so you need to maintain it in a hygienic state to ensure that food is stored safely. If you've pests or rodents, you'll need to take special care to ensure everything is put away and there's nothing for creatures to eat.

Daily

- Empty and stack the dishwasher as many times as needed to clean all the dishes.
- Hand wash and drain if not put away items that don't fit in the dishwasher.
- Hang or replace used tea towels.
- Wipe the counters, and put all the ingredients away. If you're a messy cook, clean the stove
- Sweep the floors, or if you're ok with it, leave crumbs for the dog.
- For brownie points, empty the kitchen bin into your main outside bin.

Weekly

- Get rid of leftovers and expired produce.

- Clean inside the microwave (or daily if you use it a lot).

Scheduled

- Clean the oven.
- Clean fridge and freezer.

Laundry

Getting the washing done varies according to your family size and how dirty your clothes and linens get.

You might choose to do a load of washing each weekday, for example, whites one day, towels another, and so on. Or you might decide to do all your washing on one day of the week.

In the good old days of manual washing machines and wringers, when sheets only came in flat, my mother used to wash the bottom sheets fortnightly and swap them for the top. With an automatic washing machine, you can wash them as often as you like, though probably at least fortnightly.

And while it's not technically washing, you might choose to schedule days for airing out pillows, quilts and other bedding.

Plus (of course) keep it neat, wipe up spills and monitor stores for restocking.

Bathrooms

I know people who thoroughly clean their bathrooms every day and others who do them once a week or once a month. To an extent, what you do depends on how dirty the people in your household get and how well you've trained them.

Daily (or as required)

- Wash or hang up the towels to dry. Towels get wet when you use them, and wet towels can be a breeding ground for mould and bacteria;

don't leave them for weeks between washes.

The current recommendation is washing every three uses. But if the user is ill, has problem acne, or is filthy, wash more frequently.

Having said that, if you've a heated towel rail and a well-ventilated bathroom, you could leave it a little longer. If your towels smell, you should definitely wash them!

- Replenish soap and toilet paper.

Weekly

- Clean bath, shower box, sinks, taps, towel rails and other fixtures.

- Mop floor.

Scheduled

- Clean windows, mirrors and light fixtures.

Toilets

Toilets can be dirty, filthy, disease-ridden rooms, depending on who's using them (for what), when, and how old they are.

Daily/Weekly (or when stubborn deposits accrue)

- Clean the bowl inside and out, the top and bottom of the seat, and the handle/button and the floor.

Scheduled

- Clean and disinfect the toilet brush.

Home Office/Study

I try to start my workday with an empty desk, so I do my office clean up when I finish for the day.

Daily (or as required)

- Tidy, wipe up spills, return used crockery to the kitchen, discard rubbish, water plants, replace dead or dying flowers.

- Put your stationery, books, and whatnot back where they belong so you can find them later.

- Get ready for a fresh start in the morning by tidying up your notes and papers. You might like to note your achievements and prepare your to-do list for tomorrow as well.

Weekly

- Clean your desk (with a cleaning product).

- Clean or dust your computer screen and peripherals.

- Do your filing, shred your confidential waste, and make sure your bills are paid.

Scheduled

- Reassess every single thing in your office and decide whether you still need it or could use the space better.

Garden/Outdoor Spaces

Like your home, your garden consists of public, private and functional spaces. There can be some overlap, for example, you're likely to hang your washing to dry in the sunniest area of your garden. This is also a space you'll want to enjoy privately as a family, as well as a public entertaining space.

These are the type of elements you need to consider when thinking about issues such as where to store your garbage in between collections.

Vehicles

Your vehicle will almost always be a private space, though as the interior can be clearly seen from the exterior, you could consider what it says about you. Even if you're not the kind of person who lovingly hand washes it every weekend, there's an amount of cleaning and maintenance that needs to take place to prolong its life as well as not embarrass you in public.

Summary

- One of the best ways to minimise housekeeping is to stop unwanted items coming into your home.
- Zone your home according to use.
- Think about your daily, weekly and scheduled tasks in terms of zoning rather than rooms.
- Clean high activity zones more often.
- Strategically open and close doors to control traffic flow.

CHAPTER 6

How: Getting It Done Effectively

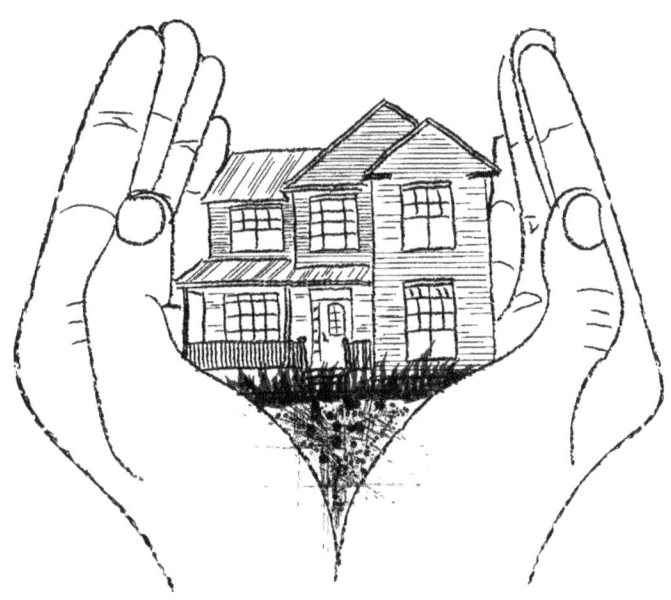

MINIMALLY VIABLE HOUSEKEEPING IS ABOUT effectiveness and efficiency; getting the right stuff done with the minimum of effort.

My first holiday after my kidney transplant was to Italy, where I naturally spent a bit of time poking about Roman ruins. I was intrigued that their design and construction assumed there would be slaves to take care of them. Not only could you enjoy the pleasures of running water in your latrines, but you wouldn't see slaves carrying urns of water to refill the cisterns because your villa included a warren of service corridors.

Similarly, historic houses like Highclere Castle required an army of domestic servants to keep the house operational, and used a bunch of service areas to hide it from view.

Given how hard I sometimes find taking care of my modern open plan home with my modern appliances, I can imagine how hopeless I might have felt when my maid gave notice for a better paying job in a factory, and I faced the prospect of doing it all myself.

Fortunately, Mrs Frederick comes to the rescue. Firstly, by reminding us that we can set whatever standards we like, and then encouraging us to take advantage of the benefits of machinery, efficient methods, and well-trained children.

You don't *have* to feel like a slave in a never-ending battle to get it all done, let alone done as well as you think it ought.

At the end of the day, you should be relaxing instead of dashing about flipping light switches, stacking and running the dishwasher, pulling clothes out of the dryer, plunking kids in front of the TV or iPad, and microwaving popcorn completely oblivious to the fact that everyone else has clocked off.

But, of course, to do this you must get your head in the right place. Getting your house in order, ship-shape Bristol fashion is a job, and like any other flexible worker, the more effective and efficient you are, the more time you've left to spend on the things that make your life worth living. And as it's your ship, you can get it done the way that best fits you and your family.

Housekeeping Philosophy

Your first step is to develop a philosophy of home care. It sounds like a lot of effort, but it's just making some decisions about how you're going to take care of your home in the future.

For example:

- It takes less time to clean a smaller house than a big one so you'll always choose a smaller.

- It takes more time to clean a lot of small items than fewer (or no) big ones so you'll minimise the ornaments and trinkets that you display.

- It takes less time to clean things that aren't there, so you'll be very careful about what new things enter your home.

- You won't do tasks that require extra effort so you'll store your tools and equipment where you can easily access them without bending, lifting, or climbing.

- It's less effort to move things once so you'll bypass the counter and stack your dishes in the dishwasher as you go.

- Tasks with low set up costs take less time and effort when done frequently so you'll sharpen knives regularly and pick up pet poo daily.

- Tasks with high set up costs take less time and effort if they're done infrequently so you'll do your ironing once a week. Or not buy clothes that need ironing.

I don't mean to imply that you must do any of this, these are just some examples to get you thinking.

Philosophical Conflicts

Now and again your housekeeping choices will conflict with your universal decisions.

For example, your core belief in protecting the environment would normally lead you to choose products and supplies that support those beliefs like reusable instead of disposable, or elbow grease over chemicals.

In general, core beliefs take priority, but at times they can be overridden by other demands. Perhaps you're having a MASSIVE party and prefer to avoid an equally massive clean up, so you'll use disposable plates, glasses, cutlery and tablecloths. (Though having said that, most hire services collect unwashed supplies because they have to rewash them anyway).

An extreme example is when winning wars is more important than not killing people.

Housekeeping is rarely the difference between life and death for humans, but now and again it will be life and death for creatures living in your house.

Your Professional Job Description

The next step is to get clear about what needs to be done, and you might find it helpful to write a job description (there's an example in Appendix C). Things to think about include:

- What is your purpose?
- What are your responsibilities?
- What knowledge and competencies do you need to fulfil them?
- What equipment do you need?
- What are your hours of work?

Minimally Viable Housekeeping

Once you've got your basics figured out, consider the constraints you operate within (e.g. the construction of your house, makeup of your family, and meal/activity times). Then you can plan your schedule and processes.

If there is too much to do, then make sure you know what your minimum essentials are and focus on them. Or think about your home's purpose again and de-clutter, rearrange and re-goal to make it simpler, quicker and easier.

Case Study: Aunt Katy (not her real name)

My Aunt Katy was a full-time nurse. She worked rotating 12-hour shifts, and at least in the early stages of her career, that was hard physical labour. She worked unsociable hours and decided that she needed to make the best of her "free" time.

She wasn't overly sentimental about her home; it was just a place to eat and sleep in between working and hanging out with her friends.

Katy chose to live in the tiniest of tiny flats with no space for clutter that took next to no time to clean. She got into the habit of putting things away as soon as she finished with them and cleaning and tidying as she went.

Any particular tasks outside that (e.g., laundry) were done before she went to bed.

She didn't worry about unexpected guests dropping in - her home was always spic and span. But she wasn't really there often enough for anyone to drop by without notice anyway.

At no time in our last few conversations did she express the desire to have done more housekeeping. She wished she'd visited Japan, gone to more museums, learned to play the piano, owned a pet, and written a book.

Can you see how her What, Why, and Who influenced her housekeeping? How can you do the same?

Effectiveness

Minimally viable housekeeping is about getting the right tasks done (effectiveness) with the least effort in the shortest amount of time (efficiency).

These days, business literature is full of the benefits of doing one thing at a time; completing the most important first.

At the same time, there's a sort of paradoxical emphasis on not getting caught up on perfection, just doing what you need to do until it's good enough for your purposes.

Here are five examples of how you can do this at home.

Essentialism

In his book *Essentialism: The disciplined pursuit of less*, Greg McKeown proposes you figure out what's essential, and focus only on getting it done. For you, that comes back to your Why. For example, if the main reason is:

- Hygiene, your essentials are going to be sterilising the house.

- Your family's health, you might leave a bit of dust and clutter but ensure meals are always carefully planned for nutritional balance.

- Other people's expectations, you might dust and vacuum every day.

Deep Work

Cal Newport, author of *Deep Work: Rules for Focused Success in a Distracted World* argues you need to set aside daily, uninterrupted time to focus on your most important task, and further develop your ability to do it well. He allows that you also need to schedule time for the little things as well.

On the assumption you've a strong motivating Why for your housekeeping, there's good reason to make time to get it done rather than trying to squeeze it into the gaps. So, schedule it, and do it deeply.

I don't mean in the moral scrubbing kind of way, I mean focus on cleaning the kitchen just enough to meet your hygiene goals, and then move onto the next task.

The One Thing

In *The One Thing: The Surprisingly Simple Truth Behind Extraordinary Results*, Gary Keller and Jay Papasan say that the way to make progress towards your long-term goals is to align your daily tasks with them. Make sure that the first thing you do each day is the most important, then do it until it's done.

You can do this at home too - when you're housekeeping, just do the housekeeping. (Do your other things in their allocated times.) Those heated conversations about housekeeping occur because you get caught up in other activities and don't get to the essentials.

Even though you're focusing on clean floors, balanced cheque accounts, and shopping lists, there's a part of your brain that's always thinking about what comes next.

Having said that, with modern appliances, you can do two tasks at once, (e.g. wash your clothes and vacuum the floors), but don't take the opportunity to mix housekeeping with your other work.

Prioritisation

Another way of looking at your day is through the analogy of Rock, Pebbles, and Sand. The story goes that a Philosophy Professor used them to demonstrate the importance of not frittering your time away on unimportant things.

You can fit it all into the jar, but only if you add them in the right order - if the sand goes in first you quickly run out of space. But if you put the rocks in first, you can add the pebbles and shake the jar until they fill the gaps. When you add the sand last, it filters through the spaces to fill the container.

The rocks are your essential tasks (to be done first). The pebbles matter, but not as much as the rocks. The sand is the small, less meaningful tasks that don't matter at all.

This model doesn't include it, but there are also tasks on your to-do list that don't matter, and you can't or won't do.

Your rocks, pebbles and sand are all reflections of your vision and purpose. Your vision of a soothing sanctuary or dimly lit library, not to mention the balance of paid and unpaid work control what's a rock and what's a pebble.

Time Budget

In her book *Work Simply: Embracing the Power of Your Personal Productivity Style*, Carson Tate argues that time is a commodity. While you can save and invest money to make more of it, you can't make more time. Once you've spent it, it's gone. It's not *as* valuable as money, it's *more* valuable.

I think it's actually worse than that because a lot of people sell their time to buy time to replace the time they're selling! And how much is that time worth anyway?

Say you're contracted to work 40 hours a week, for 48 weeks a year, for $50,000. An hour of your time is worth $26.04 [($50,000 ÷ 48 weeks) ÷ 40 hours]. You actually receive less than that because you've got taxes to pay.

You probably receive a lot less than that, because you work unpaid overtime - a single extra hour a day drops your rate to $23.15. An extra two and you're down to $20.83.

If you've been bragging about your 80-hour week, your time is worth $13.02. Are you selling yourself too cheap?

Tate suggests budgeting your time, just as you budget your money. The system I recommend is planning what you spend, share, and save based on your vision of the future.

In Chapter Two: Why Do Housekeeping I used the example of a happy future in a clean and comfortable home, married to a wonderful life partner, with angelic kids or pets who adore you. So, let's take a look at how a 24-hour day might fall out.

We'll start with sleep. Many people get by with five hours, but seven to nine results in better long-term health outcomes, so let's budget on a solid eight hours. And we'll work no more than an eight-hour day. Which leaves eight hours.

Your workday doesn't include your commute, so let's take two hours off that, leaving six. Say another two for getting everyone organised in the morning, and a little time to get changed and let go when you get home leaves you four hours.

Four hours to clean your house, prepare a healthy and delicious meal, and spend quality time bonding with your family.

Or attend a class so you can get a better job and charge more for your time.

Or do something to benefit your community.

Summary

- Effectiveness is about doing the right stuff.
- Knowing what the right stuff is makes all the difference.
- Developing a housekeeping philosophy, or foundation decisions about home care helps control the work.
- Write yourself a job description to constrain your activities.
- Develop a time budget and a perfect day framework.

CHAPTER 7

How: Getting It Done Efficiently

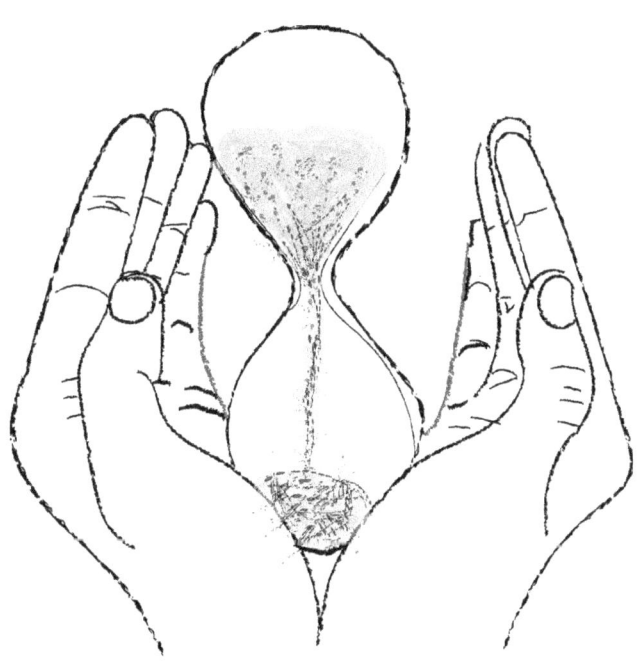

EFFICIENCY IS GETTING THE MOST done with the least amount of waste, and in the housekeeping context, we're talking about time. Just like the business context, changing systems, standardising practices, and scheduling can increase efficiency. It doesn't matter how simple or complex your household is, you can still benefit from efficiency gains.

Standardisation

Standardisation is the process of developing and implementing an agreed standard. The size of your chocolate bar is one possible outcome of standardisation, as is government regulation of environmental emissions or your high school certificate.

The idea dates back to 1776 when Adam Smith (1729 - 1790) recognised the efficiency benefits of standardisation and specialisation. Focusing on pin makers, he saw you could make more pins (and money) if semi-skilled workers made parts of the pin than one skilled craftsman made the whole pin. That's one person making the shafts, another the heads, and a third putting them together.

This also meant that customers could buy pins when they needed them rather than commissioning their manufacture.

If efficiency and effectiveness is the big picture view of minimally viable housekeeping, then standardisation is the small picture view. Rather than looking at your Why, it gets down to your process, and how you can leverage your working conditions to further increase efficiency.

According to Charles Duhigg, author of *The Power of Habits,* one potential benefit of standardisation is that it helps habit formation. What you see (or smell), triggers your routine, and because your brain is busy doing important things, you just follow the routine without thinking about it.

At its conclusion, you're rewarded by the satisfaction of a job well done. Or more likely, a cup of coffee and a sit-down, perhaps flicking through a nice glossy magazine.

As long as the conditions remain standard at any rate (which is why we lose the plot when we go on vacation).

And this means that you can set up triggers for your family so they do things like put their dirty clothes in a hamper ready for washing or their unwanted but still serviceable belongings in a "Giving Bin" so you can donate them.

So far so good, but remember the people you live with can trigger your housekeeping habits by leaving cues (e.g., empty coffee cups) lying about as well. So, if you're keen to cut down your effort, you need to notice when your habits kick in.

Let's look at a hotel maid service as an example:

- **Standard Operations:** A hotel maid cleans 15 - 30 rooms in an eight-hour shift (not counting breaks). That's 15 - 30 minutes per room! To get it all done, they use a super efficient step-by-step process that guides them from the first operational task to the last, ensuring each room gets the same quality of clean.

- **Standard Conditions:** While they appear to be designed for visitor comfort, hotel rooms are generally designed to ensure the maid's efficiency is not impeded - the more rooms they can get through, the more rooms you can let and the more money you can make. For example, the furniture is laid out so the maid circles from the door, round the room back to the door. It's is all the same height, with little clutter that needs to be moved for cleaning. They have all the tools and supplies right there in their cart when they need them.

- **Standard Practice:** The standard practice brings together the operations and conditions and adds in a schedule and quality standards (e.g., tightly fitted, smooth crease free sheets). It's a bit like a cake recipe, detailing the order of activity, the tools required, and the time allowed for each step.

While your minimally viable housekeeping doesn't have to achieve the standard you'd expect at a six-star hotel, you can minimise your time commitment by standardising your operations and conditions at home.

When businesses look at standardisation, they'll often start by reducing tasks to their component processes and redeveloping them to minimise effort and maximise efficiency. They do this by completing time and motion studies.

Time and Motion Studies

A Time and Motion Study is exactly what it sounds like: watching someone doing a task, and timing how long it takes. At the end of the observation, you change the conditions and operations in the hope of improving efficiency.

In the paid workplace, there can be issues increasing productivity regardless of the cost to the worker, but I'm assuming you're studying yourself, so you'll be taking your health and safety into account.

This does seem like a lot of effort just to get your house clean, but you're spending time discovering the most efficient way of achieving the outcome you want. You'll save time later with more accurate scheduling.

That might be the last thing on your mind, but how often have you started a task you thought would take a couple of hours and ended up losing most of an angst-ridden day to it? Like the infamous weekend garage/shed clean up.

Case Study: Hand Washing Dishes

I *know* it's not often anyone hand washes dishes anymore, and when they do, it's the big awkward stuff it's not worth running the dishwasher for.

But it makes an easily relatable example of the different steps (scraping, stacking, washing, rinsing, drying and putting away) that make up an operation we consider a single task. Increasing the efficiency of each step increases the efficiency of the entire process.

If you were doing this yourself, you'd need to conduct several trials under different conditions, timing each step of each trial. Luckily for us, Mrs Frederick's already done it, and her extensive 1923 trials suggest:

- The sink height should be comfortable for the person washing the dishes.

- The sink should be deep enough to avoid overflow.

- Right-handers should stack dirty dishes on the right of the sink and drain clean on the left (wash with the right hand and lay down with the left) Left handers stack on the left and drain on the right.

- Thoroughly scraping dishes reduces washing time.

- Dishes dry quicker on a drainer that separates them than stacked on a flat surface.

- A group of similarly shaped dishes can be washed quicker than different shaped dishes.

- Sitting lessens fatigue but doesn't increase speed.

- Scalding or rinsing dishes on the drainer with boiling water takes less time than hand drying (and is more hygienic).

- Storing dishes near the sink saves time putting them away.

If you conducted your own trials, in terms of process you might find:

- Your water gets too greasy too quickly, so you'll clean your dishes more thoroughly with a plate scraper before you wash them. You'll start with the cleanest first.

- Soap suds congeal on your dishes, so you'll use less soap and rinse with hot water.

- Your dishes may not dry adequately, so you'll rinse with hot water and try different ways of stacking them.

In terms of conditions:

- The drainer may not be on the correct side of the sink for your process, but a wheeled trolley is not only an effective surface but a convenient method of transporting the dishes to their storage area

- The countertops are too low for practical splash free use, so you'll wash your dishes in a basin that rests on another upside-down basin.

- The kitchen sink is too shallow to comfortably fit your pots, so you'll buy smaller ones, but in the meantime, you'll use your laundry trough and see what effect that has. Or maybe take them outside and wash them on the lawn at the same time as the dog.

- Your wall-mounted dish rack is too high to comfortably reach, so you'll have it lowered.

- Or removed and replaced with one that sits on the counter or drainer.

- Your dish towels are stored inconveniently far away from the sink, so you'll find somewhere closer to put them.

- Your dish cupboards are inconveniently far away, so you'll relocate them or use a trolley.

The important thing is not to change the way you complete your tasks to accommodate the quirks of your home but to adjust your home to fulfil your efficiency needs.

And to keep notes so when it's time to renovate or buy a new home, you can include your needs in the construction.

Standardising Housekeeping

We all have tasks that seem to take forever, and these are the ones that will probably benefit the most from standardisation.

It's likely that the physical elements of housekeeping (cooking, cleaning, caring and property management) will take up the bulk of your housekeeping time.

These processes consist of many tasks, for example:

- Cleaning involves dusting, sweeping, mopping (or scrubbing), and polishing.

- Caring can include lifting, washing, toileting, medicating, plumping pillows and so on.

It's physical labour, and each step requires muscular adjustments. Perhaps you need to activate your core so you can lift heavy loads. Or balance on your toes so you can reach high items. Or bend to pick items off the floor.

This range of movement can be helped or hindered by your room layout.

Standard Operations

The most efficient clean moves top down, then dry to wet. Your workflow proceeds from ceiling to lights to pictures and mirrors, to ornaments, tables and horizontal surfaces, then furniture, rugs and flooring. Debris is dusted to the floor, gets sucked up by the vacuum, followed by mopping.

And like our maid, it's more efficient to clean in a circuit than to trot backwards and forwards - clockwise for right-handers and anti-clockwise for left. However, if cleaning is part of your exercise plan, keep trotting!

Hotel check-in and out schedules being what they are, maids have to clean room by room, cleaning each on in a circuit starting with the bedroom and ending with the bathroom.

- Bend and pull to strip the bed, bend, lift and carry the linen, towels and rubbish to the cart.
- Bend, lift, push and pull to remake the bed.
- Reach and move your arms dusting from top to bottom.
- Bend and push the vacuum wand forwards and pull backwards.
- Bend, reach, push and pull while cleaning the bathroom.
- Use back and arms to swing the mop from side to side.

But just as office workers lose efficiency when they change tasks (e.g., answering the phone while reconciling accounts), maids lose efficiency when they change tasks too.

Not only are they making the mental and physical effort of swapping; warming up and readjusting the muscles for each task in each room, they're carrying their tools room to room too. The continual swapping not only takes up time but adds a physical load that can be more tiring than the tasks themselves.

At home, cleaning by task eliminates the swapping. For example, dusting all the rooms, then vacuuming all the rooms. Similarly, any specialised or irregular tasks like washing windows. It also gives you the opportunity to store your task related tools as you finish each one.

Your process might look like this:

- Collect your tools (dusters, vacuum, bin and mop) and leave them outside the first room.

- Starting in the first room, pull back the curtains and open the windows, and do the same in the rest of the rooms in your circuit.

- Beginning again at room one, dust (top down), put the rubbish in your bin, and the same for the rest of your circuit. If your cupboard is nearby, put your dusting tools away, if not, leave them outside room one.

- Vacuum all rooms and put the machine away/leave it outside room one.

- Mop rooms as appropriate.

- Put your tools and supplies away.

- Close windows, adjust curtains, and close doors as appropriate.

Standard Conditions

The main reason housekeeping was such hard, physical labour and took such a long time was because most homes didn't have running water, electricity or gas delivered to their homes. Everything was done by hand, from carrying your buckets to and from the well, to growing your own food, to keeping the wood fire going all day so you could cook dinner.

By comparison, we have it easy, but we can make it easier by taking advantage of all the tips and tricks to make physical tasks easier and therefore quicker.

You already do this to a point by arranging furniture, centralising storage and getting efficient appliances. You just need to be a little more methodical to ensure you get the best possible results with the least possible effort. Or as business people call it, leverage a small investment for a larger return.

Remember, standard conditions aren't just effective for you; you can use them to trigger housekeeping behaviours in those sharing your home. Every family is different, but things like basketball hoops over the linen basket, submarine stickers in the toilet, and bowls of fruit on the counter can encourage the formation of habits that reduce your housekeeping effort.

Layout

It's easy to think we could just replicate a hotel room layout to improve our cleaning efficiency, but hotel rooms are essentially single-purpose rooms where one or two people sleep (and bathe) for a night or two. They don't take into account daytime activities, long-term storage or your personal taste.

When you start thinking about a room's layout, the most important factor has to be its purpose(s). While your bedroom's purpose is still primarily for sleeping, you may also read, exercise, mend clothes, craft, watch TV, listen to music, pay bills, run your business, and so on.

So how exactly do you manage all that?

Julie Morgenstern, author of *Organizing from the Inside Out: The foolproof system for organizing your home, your office, and your life* suggests starting with the "Kindergarten Model."

Divide the room into relevant zones then rearrange the furniture and store all the appropriate tools and supplies in the zones you'll be using them in.

Not just anyhow, but in labelled containers that are just the right size for their contents. She suggests this approach makes it quick and easy to clean up when you finish a task, so it's worth thinking about how you can use this in areas you want to inspire others to do their share.

When it comes to laying out your zones, you could use the "Cockpit Principle" described by Liz Davenport in *Order From Chaos: A six-step plan for organizing yourself, your office, and your life*.

The principle states that you only keep essentials nearby; daily within hand's reach, weekly arms reach, and monthly somewhere in the room. Anything you use less often can be in long-term storage somewhere else.

You should still consider a process circuit that permits your dominant hand the most freedom of movement (clockwise for right-handers, and anticlockwise for lefties) as well as making it easy for you to work top down, and dry to wet. But it's more important that the rooms in your home reflect their purpose.

Storage

One of the useful things about having designated places for storing your tools and supplies close to the place you use them is making them the start and finish of your operational circuits:

- Food in the kitchen.
- Linens near the bedrooms:
- Cleaning tools and supplies centrally.

Ideally, storage will be big enough to fit all your bits and bobs, so you don't need to check different places. For example, your cleaning cupboard needs to be tall enough for mops and brooms, and wide enough to include your vacuum and buckets. Having a shelf for cleaning products and hooks for your tool bag, apron, and small tools like dusters will be handy too.

Frequently used items should be stored at waist height, rarely used up high, and in between below - ideally only rarely used items below knee or above shoulder height. Unless you can install a "library" ladder or have a very stable stool.

The doors should slide, or open outwards. If you can rig up lights inside walk-ins, you'll be able to see what's going on.

Make sure your shelves are not so deep you can't easily reach the back of them, though you might find it useful if the waist height shelf is deeper, perhaps standard counter depth.

And it's best if you can store clean items (e.g., bed linen and towels), separate from the dirty.

Efficient Equipment

When was the last time you upgraded your tools and equipment? It's possible you're using your old reliable machines because they're still operational. But you could be wasting time and effort moving them around your home.

Like vacuuming for example. You're lifting a heavy piece of equipment out of your cupboard, pushing, pulling and dragging it around your home, emptying, unplugging and replugging it as you go, before lifting it back into the cupboard. It could be the most laborious task you do on any given day, and I imagine it makes you feel like you've achieved something.

But a new lightweight cordless vacuum would save you time and effort storing and using it, despite having to empty it more often. Or if your cleaning schedule is different rooms each day, you could be emptying it just before you store it.

Plus, with the advances in technology, it may clean more thoroughly than your old machine. You could do it daily, but you wouldn't need to.

Similarly, modern dishwashers (and detergents) will thoroughly clean dishes without you having to rinse them. You can also get fridges and freezers that defrost themselves, and clothes washers that choose the water level and spin cycle. Vacuum cleaners, air conditioners, and air filters with high-efficiency particulate air (HEPA) filters that remove most of the particles that may exacerbate respiratory conditions.

Like domestic buildings, most household appliances are designed by men who don't use them, so bear that in mind when you shop for equipment. It must be easy for YOU to use, with a minimum of bending, stretching, and lifting so check the size, scale, shape of the machine as well as the location of the levers, buttons, handles and knobs. If you're not happy with the ease and comfort of use, just don't buy it, because you won't use it.

There's no point buying equipment that's difficult to use. Or takes more time and effort to clean and maintain than you save by using (unless the end result is so remarkable that you willingly make the sacrifice). Also, don't buy damaged or ill-made products with rough or sharp edges that may injure you.

Make sure you understand the requirements of your appliances, and the differences between the models so you'll get the one that best matches your needs. How often will you have to empty the vacuum? Is it light enough for you to handle on your own? How much bedding can the clothes washer take? Will it fit in the space you've prepared for it?

And then, of course, to ensure your appliance's long-term viability, site them appropriately, care for them properly, and use them correctly.

Case Study: Doing the Laundry

Let's think about the process first:

- **Collect:** Going from room to room, bending and lifting, and carrying it back to the laundry.

- **Sort:** Lifting it onto the counter or emptying it on the floor, spreading it out, and creating piles according to treatment.

- **Wash:** Lifting it into the machine, adding detergents and conditioning agents.

- **Dry:** Lifting or pulling it out of the machine into your basket. Lift your basket onto a table or counter. Step up onto your stool or ladder, bend to pick up a garment, flick it to unravel it and place it in the dryer or on an internal washing line. Or lift and carry the basket to a washing line, place it on the ground nearby, bend to pick up a garment, flick it to unravel it and reach to peg it on the line.

- **Fold:** Pull each garment off the line, fold and drop it into the basket, bend to pick up and carry the basket back to the laundry. Or step up onto your stool or ladder and pull a garment loose from the dryer, flick it to loosen it, fold and lay in the basket. Or drag everything into the basket, empty onto the table or counter, pick up a garment, flick it, lay it flat and fold it.

- **Iron** (if you do it): Dampen and hang clothes. Open ironing board, collect iron and plug it in to heat up. Collect water and pour into the steam compartment. When it's hot, pick a garment and push the iron over it. Set the iron aside and rehang the garment.

- **Put away:** Collect all your clean, ironed and folded clothing and carry it to the room it belongs, bend and reach to put them in the drawers or closet. Make as many trips as you need.

Now you can start improving your conditions:

- Arrange the room in a process circuit.

- You may not be able to drop your counters as they are probably held up by built-in storage, but you may be able to install a platform that raises you a little higher.

- Buy a waist height trolley to put your basket on and use it for collecting, drying, folding, ironing and putting away the laundry.

- Install your washer and dryer at waist height to avoid bending and lifting.

- If you own a two or more-storey house and can afford to, install a laundry chute that empties onto your laundry sorting counter.

- Get your family to pick up and deliver their clothes to the laundry.

Standard Practice

You'll need to experiment with your process, conditions and schedule until you end up with something practical for you. Then write down the steps with a note of your timing so that you can estimate how long the tasks and overall process takes. This becomes your Standard Practice; you can give it to others as a job description or challenge yourself to improve your times. It's all about getting the right tasks done at the right time with the right tools nearby.

Case Study: Kitchen Standard Practice

Most kitchen tasks break down into one of two processes: food preparation or post-meal cleanup.

Kitchen Operations

The process of preparing scrambled eggs on toast involves:

Preparing

- Collecting your ingredients from the fridge and pantry and taking them to the countertop or a table.
- Collecting your utensils from storage and taking them to the countertop or a table.
- Beating the eggs.
- Slicing the bread.

Cooking

- Collecting your cookware and utensils from storage and taking them to the stove.
- Taking the eggs to the stove and cooking them.
- Taking the bread to the toaster and toasting it.

Serving

- Collecting a plate and cutlery and taking it to the countertop or a table.
- Bringing the toast to the countertop, putting it on the plate and maybe buttering it.
- Bringing the eggs to the countertop and putting them on the toast.

- Adding salt and pepper or other condiments to taste.
- Taking the plate to the table to eat.

Once you've eaten, it's time to clean up which involves:
Removing
- Bringing used crockery, cutlery, and foodstuffs back to the kitchen.

Washing
- Scraping uneaten food into the bin.
- Stacking the dishwasher.
- Hand washing the cookware.
- Wiping down the countertops and stove.

Putting Away
- Returning foodstuffs to storage.
- Returning plates and cutlery to storage.
- Returning cookware to storage.
- Hanging up tea towels.

This could involve a zig-zag path from cupboard to countertop to stove, back to the countertop, then to a table to the bin to sink, back to the countertop, and finally back to the cupboard.

Kitchen Conditions

Modern kitchens have become relatively spacious multipurpose rooms where people cook, eat, hang out, watch TV, pay bills, do homework or craft work, as well as general multipurpose storage. In some ways, it's like a return to the single room dwellings our ancestors lived in.

Regardless of what you do in them, most are designed by architects or builders with the goal of maximising their efficiency, not yours. If you're not in the position to renovate the space to suit your needs, you'll have to think about how you use the space to increase your efficiency within its limitations.

If you operationalise Morgenstern's zones, you'll get preparation, cooking, serving, and clean up, so you'll want these in a circuit that reduces your steps, movement and time.

If you're right-handed, this starts with food storage to the left of food preparation, moving right to the stove and further right to serving. For the cleanup, you'll need a workspace to the right of the sink and drainage to the left (opposite for left).

Adding Davenport's cockpit, your preparation zone will include your daily utensils and tools, probably stored in easily reachable containers on the counter. Like a coffee area with kettle/coffee maker, cups and supplies.

Your weekly use might be in drawers or cupboards within reach of a step or two; for example, recipe books, blenders or roasting pans. Everything else (e.g., food processors, pudding basins or sushi mat) can be further away in places you need to bend or stand on a stool to reach.

Similarly, cookware and supplies in the cooking zone, serving in the serving zone, and scrapers, dish soap and cloths in the cleanup. Your serving and clean up zones will probably share the dish storage space.

Additionally, you'll need zone specific lighting; ideally to one side of you, so you're not working in your own shadow. Plus, adequate ventilation to ensure good oxygen levels and extraction fans to carry away cooking odours.

The floor should be of a substance that's easy to clean and comfortable to stand on. A curved baseboard is easy to clean

Minimally Viable Housekeeping

and prevents muck from getting caught in the cracks. Kitchen decoration and fittings should be chosen according to the ease and completeness of cleaning. Choose colours to enhance the quality of light as well as their attractiveness.

If you're the kind of person who uses small appliances more for decoration than for food preparation, consider how much:

- Time you could save by not moving them to clean (or more likely cleaning around), and
- Space you'd have to work in if you stored them in cupboards or on shelves.
- Money you could save with less expensive decorative elements. Bowl of fruit perhaps?

Kitchen Practice

Obviously, every meal you prepare will be different, but having your kitchen zoned and laid out for the process will reduce the amount of time you need to get it done. It'll also make it easier to cost outsourcing some activities.

Efficiency Methodologies

Six Sigma

Six Sigma is essentially a statistical method for examining processes and developing improvements leading to a more effective and efficient system.

As it's more about operations than conditions, it can be a useful way to frame your thinking about what makes an efficient housekeeping practice.

It's usually integrated into a manufacturing process to reduce product defects, but in housekeeping, I'd recommend it as a periodic stand-alone project. There are some variations, but the basic process is:

1. **Define Your Goals:** While your overarching goal is minimally viable housekeeping, this broadness makes it hard to focus in on the best way to achieve it. Focusing your thinking with your Why, and analysing a particular room or task gives better results. For example, getting everyone out of the house, arriving at work or school with full bellies, lunch, and all the supplies they need for the day.

2. **Measure Critical to Quality Characteristics:** This has two parts; the result you want, and what's blocking it. To gather the data, you'll time each step of your morning operation, noting the causes of delay. For a richer data set, you could monitor for a week or more to examine variations between days. For our morning routine example, you might note the lure of the snooze button, that child #2's gym clothes from last week are still in their kit bag, you ran out of cornflakes, and so on.

3. **Analyse Your Results:** Hopefully, you've a good list of issues and delays. Consider how each blocks you and rank them from biggest to smallest impact. Too many snoozes is probably a biggie! Good job not murdering child #2, though it came close for a minute there. Running out of cornflakes not so much of a problem because you had toast instead, but it added confusion and delay.

4. **Design Alternatives:** During the previous steps, you probably had intuitive flashes of solution. Start a list with these, and brainstorm as many other options as you can. It doesn't matter how far-fetched or expensive they seem, you're just collating options. Some will be simple fixes (e.g., back up cornflakes). Others take more effort, like training children to put their gym clothes in the wash. Now and again, especially when you've already had several runs through the Six Sigma process, you'll need to think more deeply and creatively. For

Minimally Viable Housekeeping

example, rearranging your day so you can all get to bed earlier and don't hit the snooze button in the morning.

5. **Do a Test Run:** Once you've got some alternatives, implement the one you think will make the most difference and do a test run to see how much closer you get. Are you close enough to leave it as is? Do you need a second solution? Would a different solution provide a better result? Would another Six Sigma round with your implemented changes bring up something more effective? Keep going until you're happy with the result. Stockpiling cornflakes alone won't make much difference, but perhaps laying the table for breakfast the night before will.

This process is a great one to run when you feel like there is more that can be done, but you don't quite know what, or where to start.

Kaizen

Kaizen is a philosophy of continuous improvement; making small changes as and when you identify improvements in the flow or process. A bit like the way you learn to make your perfect cup of coffee - over time you fine-tune the brands and amounts of ingredients, the tools and appliances you use, and the time it takes.

Lean

The Lean Methodology is a more complicated version of Kaizen. It's often used at the same time as Six Sigma, but it's not the same thing.

Six Sigma focuses on improving the product, and Lean on reducing waste (whether that's time, money, or other resources). Six Sigma works from the business point of view and

Lean from the customer. Six Sigma is project-based, whereas Lean is a continuous improvement programme.

1. **Identify Value:** Find out what the customer wants. Getting back to the morning routine example, this is probably the same as you; to get to work/school with a full belly, lunch, and all the supplies needed for the day. Sometimes it will not be as obvious, and you might need to ask them. In the household context, you might have to impose what they need rather than giving them what they want.

2. **Map the Value Stream:** Identify each step in the process and get rid of the ones that don't create value. This would be the ones where you're shouting at people to get out of bed, arguing about sandwich fillings, and trying to find school bags.

3. **Create Flow:** Make sure the steps occur in the sequence that delivers the best value. While things like making the perfect cup of coffee will almost always follow a tight sequential flow, getting people out of the house in the morning has a longer, more complicated process that stretches out over a week or more. You need to make sure gym clothes are washed and ready on sports day, everyone knows where their bags are and that sandwiches and gym clothes make it into them. You also need to manage your family, making sure they are out of bed, washed and ready to leave the house on time.

4. **Establish Pull:** In business, it's more complicated, but in your home, it's moving from a system where you push everyone around, to one where they draw on you instead. Like Netflix - when you want it, they deliver it. For your morning routine, it's when you're in the kitchen enjoying a quiet, peaceful coffee and

your family troops in one by one, wanting breakfast which is laid our ready to go.

5. **Get Better:** As your process improves, go back to the beginning and continue to eliminate waste until it's all gone.

In reality, it's not a nice clear cycle, and it will take time to establish, but it will take some of the stress out of your day.

Outsourcing

One way to avoid a lot of the housekeeping drama is to outsource it, either by hiring an ongoing housekeeper to do it all, or services to clean or garden on a regular or ad hoc basis.

Hiring someone to complete the tasks for you will eliminate some relationship friction but puts you in the position of monitoring the quality of someone else's labour. Which means that you need to be very clear about your expectations.

Schedules of assigned tasks and standard hours are just as important for those who work for you as for you. You'll use the same process to determine their daily and weekly tasks, special tasks, rest breaks and time off. Plus, their start, finish and break times, as well meet with you about their daily routine, special tasks and arrangements for holidays and time off.

Summary

- Efficiency is getting the most done with least waste.
- Households can benefit from efficiency gains as much as businesses do.
- Develop standard practices.
- Embrace continuous improvement.
- Consider outsourcing.

Conclusion

HOUSEKEEPING IS NEVER-ENDING. IT DOESN'T matter where you look, there's always something that needs doing. Whether that's putting someone's abandoned cup in the dishwasher, cleaning the toilet bowl or putting food on the table. There's no changing that.

But it doesn't have to be you that does it all.

And if for some reason it does, consider what proportion of your precious non-renewable time you want to put towards it.

Just because we've talked about daily and weekly schedules doesn't mean you have to use them. If your other work has a different cycle, it might be easier to work within that.

For example, when I'm working on a new book, I don't actually spend a lot of time at my desk. I'm still working through my ideas, and as I'm not ready to commit to paper, I tend to do other things with my hands. That's the time I dust, refold the clothes in my drawers and move all the furniture to vacuum the dog hair out from underneath it.

But when I get towards the end of a book (like now), that's when we tend to run out of coffee mugs, clean underpants and dog food. As well as trying to capture the last few words dripping out of my fingers, I'm managing illustrators, cover designers, book interiors, indexers, editors, and so on. I need to keep all that moving, so I don't run out of their time or my own. And by that point I generally just want the thing to be over.

Which means that I tend to "Spring Clean" between projects, partly to help clean and reset my brain and partly to get the house looking "decent" again. My project cycle guides my choice of a relatively uncluttered home and a Lean housekeeping process, though goodness knows this old house could do with some more storage!

My desire to write books is why I'm continually maximising my writing time by minimising my housekeeping time. It's why the clothes washer goes on at 6.30 am, and the dishwasher at 10.30 pm. It's why I leap out of bed at 2 am to let my poor old dog out, and why DB now wears non-iron work shirts (he also chooses not to iron).

I don't want you to think that I don't believe housekeeping is important, because I do. It's just that you only have 24 single-use hours each day, and you have to use them wisely.

Like mine, your days, weeks, and months can only ever be used once. Every time you say yes to one activity, you say no to a whole host of others.

Some days will be chaotic, others calm. Now and again you'll devote all your energy towards a single goal, whether that's redecorating your guest room, or getting a new product ready for market. Periodically you'll have more than enough time to catch up.

The main thing is to know that what you do with your time is your choice - only you have the right to tell you what to do with your time. Whatever activities you choose, choose them guilt free. Don't feel bad when other things take precedence, that's just the nature of life.

I think it'd be nice if others did more around the house. But I understand that driving to an office takes more time and energy than walking between my desk and the kitchen.

I want you to have the ability to make the best choice about what to do with your available time, at that time.

Sometimes it will be easy, and there will be no obstructions between you and what you want to get done. Other times you'll be working against your own inclinations.

I hope this book gives you options. I hope it helps you improve your efficiency and effectiveness when you do choose to do the housekeeping.

Appendix A: For Those Working at Home

While undertaking paid work from home has its problems, I don't miss overcrowded, overheated, stuffy, flu-ridden offices at all. I do, however, miss spending time with people, daily cafe visits, and guilt-free commuting idleness.

Some of my friends think I'm lucky, because not only do I save money on transport, takeout coffee, lunches, dry-cleaning and childcare, there's no commute, no boss, no interruptions and no dress code.

But among other downsides, I've got sky-high utility bills, more clutter than you can poke a stick at, and door-to-door salesmen to contend with.

Happily, as a woman, my home is already a place of work. We tend to have less trouble adjusting to paid work at home than our poor husbands who see "home" as a separate place to "work". A place where their clean clothes, hot dinners, and freshly bathed children arrive miraculously on schedule. Like some kind of elaborate wind-up toy.

But it's not all pyjamas and fluffy slippers, it's paid work, and with that comes responsibility.

The information that follows is rife with contradiction, but working at home for money is contradictory these days, even though it was once common.

And in any case, your thoughts and feelings about paid work at home will change day to day, and some days are easier than others.

Work

Working at home can be great - you've no office distractions and can get a lot more done than you otherwise might.

Your local supervisory boss (you) is generally very lenient. She lets you take time off to get your hair done, go to yoga class and meet friends for lunch. She'll also let you work in the garden when it's sunny, at the local coffee shop when you feel lonely, and take a day off when you're just not feeling it at all.

But she's generally not very pushy, and you may find that hours or days go by without you achieving much. At some point, you have to take control and get started. And sometimes, you have to intervene and stop.

Motivation

For some weird reason, it's a lot easier to get motivated to go to work when you have to leave the house. You don't have to fight to make yourself get up and go. You're already committed by the time you're fully awake - your brain is already there.

To succeed at home, you need to bring the same level of motivation and commitment to getting to work, plus the discipline to sit down and just get on with it. Motivation gets you started, but discipline and self-control keep you going.

Motivation can be carrot (positive) or stick (negative). A carrot is generally some kind of reward, for example, I'll get this done and finish up for the day. The stick might be the threat of losing your job (or income).

My motivation arrives in the form of goals and targets with schedules that keep me moving forward. Because writing a book takes a fair amount of time, I find that motivation comes and goes, so I have to focus on the end goal. Sometimes I'm so excited I can't wait to get started, and other times it's sheer bloody-mindedness that keeps me on track. Starting is the hard part, but once I get started, it's easier to keep going.

And something that helps you get started is the same habits and practices as you put together for the housekeeping.

Standard Practice

Your paid work can benefit from standard practices as much as your housekeeping. In fact, you could look at your day overall as a sequence of standard practices slipping from housekeeping, to paid work, to housekeeping and into leisure time.

Operations

In the same way as leaving home for work, it helps to set up an entry point. While your paid work probably doesn't involve cleaning in a circle, you need to set up some kind of loop to get the process started.

For example, my friend Katie dresses for work, leaves the house and takes a walk around the block to go to work. When she reaches the house, she treats it as entering her workplace. And the reverse at the end of the day.

Once you reach your office, you'll need to open loops that lead into your paid working day. For example, many office workers turn their computers on, then hang up their coats, visit the bathroom and make coffee while it powers up and connects to the network. You can do the same.

Similarly, you can break your day into task-based work units, by stretching, visiting the bathroom, going for a short walk or fetching another drink. Not to mention eating lunch. You can use the Ideal Day to plan this.

When you're alone, it's easy to either not get started, or to get so caught up in what you're doing you lose track of time (resulting in those heated housekeeping discussions). For some, the Pomodoro technique of timed work units can help alleviate this. Or the opposite of Pomodoro - set your timer, so you don't get carried away on social media or your breaks.

If you need help, consider a software solution like Workpace. It's actually an ergonomic program that encourages you to take breaks and demonstrates exercises and stretches, but you can set it to lock you out, so you've no choice but to take the required break. (It's harder to be motivated about taking breaks when you're not being paid to turn up).

Planning your days and weeks in line with your goals allows you to schedule and complete larger pieces of work throughout your working week. I plan my workday using an Ideal Day template. It's a big block of time within my housekeeping day, so I have flexibility where I need it. When I need to take a half day off for an appointment or other activity, I try to add it back in through the rest of the week.

We talked a little bit about chronotypes in Chapter Four: When Does it Get Done?, and you can use this to your full advantage; when you're sharp whether that's in the morning, or the night you can do your paperwork. And when you're less sharp whatever time that happens you can do housekeeping.

For example, you might feel a bit sleepy after lunch so you could do a bit of cleaning to get your energy levels back up before you go back and do another hour of paid work.

You'll generally get the best results if you don't allow the housekeeping to overlap or intermingle your work day. But having said that, sometimes when you're thinking deeply you might need something to aid your thought process. In an office, you might make yourself a coffee, chat with your colleagues or do your filing. At home, it could be useful to do some minor housekeeping instead, just remember you're at work and act accordingly.

If you need to track your working time, you could consider setting up a timesheet spreadsheet or use an app such as RescueTime, that monitors your computer usage. You can track and control which programs and websites you spend time on, and decide whether this is in line with what you want. You can also set targets, nominate sites and applications as productive or unproductive, and categorise the activities you do to get an overall idea of how productive you are.

Don't just abandon your desk at the end of your working day. Before you finish up for the day, put your work away, and tidy your desk. Some people like to write a short to-do list with their top priorities, so they know where to start the next day. Others like to leave half done tasks ready to pick up.

One of my friends has a deadbolt and open/closed sign installed on her home office door, and when she leaves, she locks up and flips the closed sign. Not only does it signal the end of her working day, but it makes it slightly more difficult to just slip in and do a little bit later.

If working at home looks to be a long-term situation, consider starting a continuous improvement project finding out how other people manage their processes and conditions and apply relevant solutions to your office.

Conditions

When you work at home, you need a place to work. It's best as a separate space where you can store your office supplies and secure your work in progress. Preferably not your dining table, your bed or in front of the television.

If you'll be telecommuting, consider what your colleagues will see, and exclude toilets, washing (clean or otherwise) and messy piles of stuff from the field of vision. (Yes, I really have seen someone's toilet [in use] during a video conference).

Even though you're working at home, you need suitable business equipment including a fast computer, scanner and printer as well as a reliable system for backing up your work.

You'll also need reliable high-speed Internet access with sufficient bandwidth to send and receive large files. Plus, knowledge about how to update it and keep it all operational. If you're working directly for a business, they should supply or subsidise your purchases.

One of the main arguments for working at home is the absence of distractions, so turn off all your notifications (e.g., email and facebook) and put your phone on silent. If you're easily distracted by social media or other apps, you could install a distraction blocker like SelfControl (for Macs), Freedom, LeechBlock, AntiSocial or FocusWriter.

If you can't work in silence, consider downloading a soundtrack of some kind. While some people prefer classical, heavy metal or meditation music, others prefer sound effects like an office or shop, busy transport hub or as I recently discovered, twelve hours of snowstorm. Don't feel obliged to choose just one, you can change them according to the work you're doing and how inspired you need to feel.

You

When you work at home, your home is also your workplace, and it can be hard to maintain boundaries between the two.

There's always the temptation to use housekeeping to avoid work, and when an idea comes to you, it's all too easy to slip into work mode. Either way, you have to choose

Balance

While my default position is that there is just life, there is a lot of balancing and rebalancing as the days and years pass by.

Minimally Viable Housekeeping

Some days you never reach equilibrium, some days you never quite get started, other days you don't get finished. But each day is a new day with the opportunity to do it better.

A while back, Confucius (551 – 479 BCE) said something along the lines of "Choose a job you love, and you will never work a day in your life." It's a thought that many people, including singer Marc Anthony, have picked up and run with.

As I see it, I don't work A day, I work EVERY day! There's always something to be done, and without an office full of lackeys, I have to do it all.

But even if I didn't, I'd still be thinking about my work - inspiration comes at the oddest moments. And that's not something I can turn off. Even if I wanted to. Which I don't.

Besides which, my desk is just a few steps away from my bed, my kitchen, my couch, etc. It's next to no drama to get up and go do some work.

But I do think it's important to be mindful. That whatever you're doing, to do it with full awareness and appreciation. When you have dinner with your family, bring all your focus, attention and gratitude to that moment. Don't think about work, check your phone or anything else, just be with and enjoy your time with them.

Which is why I recommend you restrict your work calls and emails to the usual business hours in your jurisdiction. When you protect other people's non-working time, they'll be more inclined to defend yours. If you contact people late at night or on weekends, you implicitly give them permission to do the same to you.

It's also why I like to buy services from people who live on the other side of the planet. I can send them information and requests and forget about it until the next day. I don't need to keep checking for responses, and neither do they. We all have our working day to think about it.

Though if you do have to work out of hours, you're at home so you can take a few hours off to spend time with your family before getting back to work later at night.

Balance is not an absolute, sometimes it leans in one direction, and sometimes the other. You'll get too much paid work done at the cost of the housekeeping, or vice versa. Or you'll get neither of them done very well.

But this is one of the reasons you've chosen to work at home - flexibility.

Health

It is also easy to forget about your health when you work at home. You might not drink enough water, eat too many snacks or skip the exercise.

One of the key issues many people don't consider is the cost of social isolation. Without interaction with others, it's easy to become the crazy pet person who's forgotten how to talk intelligently with grown-up humans.

If you don't have work-related meetings to attend, get out of the house now and again. Go for a walk in the sunshine, run some errands and interact with people. Much better to be the crazy bus stop lady who talks to strangers.

It's also common to feel guiltier about taking care of yourself as you think you *should* be working. If not your paid work, then your housekeeping. But I think it's more important to make time to take care of yourself, whether that's exercise, a home facial or a massage.

Relationships

When you're juggling paid and unpaid work, relationships can get a bit fraught. Especially if you aren't getting positive reinforcement from outside your home.

Minimally Viable Housekeeping

Aside from interruptions, you may also have to deal with jealousy, impatience and the assumption that you're either stupid or lazy. Or both!

Family

If it comes to a choice, relationships with your immediate family (partner and kids) have to come first because they have the most significant impact on your life overall. If they're happy, you'll be happy and less distracted at your work.

Potentially, your kids will be the most time consuming, so consider whether you want to send them to their grandparents or childcare now and again. Kids who are stuck at home with their parents often think this is a treat.

One of my friends converted her games room into an office so she could put desks for her kids in there. When they get home from school, they do their homework in there while she gets some of her non-urgent non-important work done.

Friends

One of the hardest things to bear is when a friend drops in when you're working towards a hard deadline, though sometimes it's hard because they don't!

When they don't understand you're *working*, and ask for favours that will take you away from your work, you might upset them when you say no. You'll probably feel bad, but remember you're working. You have a schedule of things you need to do, and if you allow other people to hijack your time, you will never have the time to do the things you *need* to do.

Having a work schedule means you can tell people when you're available as well as when you're not.

Colleagues

Without a presence in the office, you will be forgotten, so it's a good idea to stay in touch with your boss and colleagues and keep them up-to-date with your progress.

Schedule regular meetings - either in person or by phone. A Skype or Zoom video conference will help manage misunderstandings because you'll be able to see the people you're meeting. If it's a social office, invite them for team lunches, or to your home now and again for meals.

Don't rely on email or your boss when you've urgent information to share. Emails are very easy to lose track of; I have around 800 unread emails in my inbox at the moment...

If you're going to miss a deadline or have some other important information to share, ring them and leave a short message or speak to them in person.

When you're missing the stimulation of other people, it's common to check your email frequently just to see if anything happened. It's also common to check because you're afraid of being left out of the loop. However, a better option is to schedule those meetings and focus on the work you have at hand.

When you're starved of company, it's easy to overshare with your colleagues. Unless you're particular friends, try to keep your conversations professional and not share information you will be embarrassed about later.

Appendix B: Housework Survey: What You Really Think

A while back, I wrote a blog post asking if there was such a thing as minimum viable housework and I set up a survey to get the results. The survey said maybe.

As you read the results, you'll guess it was mostly women who completed it, but interestingly, the mix of age groups was more or less even across the pool. And the concerns expressed were more or less the same across the age groups too. It seems that the more things change, the more they stay the same.

Housework Survey Says: It's Not Enough

Admittedly I didn't have a huge response, but I was surprised that 40% felt they weren't spending enough time on home/care cleaning. Mind you, the same proportion said it was just enough. Very few thought they were doing too much.

I found the reasons why we clean particularly interesting.

- More people were worried about what other people think than were concerned about rodents, bugs and germs!

- Personal reasons were only slightly more important than bugs –more in the sense of not feeling bad than for feeling good about it.

There were a couple of lovely outliers though;

- Feeling lighter when the house is cleaner, and
- Wanting dignity and beautiful surroundings.

Housework Survey Says: Cleaning is Not Cleaning

Almost all respondents spent most of their time tidying up, washing dishes and clothes, though not all of us think of this as cleaning, and these tasks aren't delegated to cleaners coming in. Very few of us dust – no real surprise there!

Housework Survey Says: Most Important Chore is Contextual

While doing the dishes was the top most important chore, I was fascinated to learn that for many respondents, the important chore is whatever has backed up the most; kitchen, bathroom or clothes.

One respondent confessed they prioritise the tasks their family are concerned about and let the others slide. I think that's a pretty good example of "If it ain't broke, don't fix it!"

Housework Survey Says: Too Busy Doing

It seems that everyone is busy doing everything – paid work, voluntary work, housework, a job on the side, studying on the side, taking care of children. The only conclusion I can come to is that no one has any time to themselves, and that has to stop! We need to make time for ourselves.

Housework Survey Says: Need Help NOW!

Many respondents commented on their desire for others in the household to do more, not wanting to nag, but not sure how else to get anything done. And while some bought in help, they felt like a failure because they couldn't manage on their own.

Others talked about how they routinised their chores, so at the very least the most important stuff gets done. And also, the opposite, leaving it until it gets bad enough to be apparent that the cleaning was done.

And after my own heart, some who use smelly products to make it seem they've done more than they actually have!

The Hotwash

I envy those who get joy and satisfaction from their cleaning – sadly, there's nothing in my survey to suggest why they're so different from the rest of us.

Perhaps they live alone, and their homes are more authentic representations of themselves. Or maybe they live in small, streamlined homes that take next to no time to care for. Or don't have basements, attics or garages stuffed with the detritus of life to hold them back.

Whatever the reason, it's something I'll be thinking more about.

Appendix C: Example Job Description

You'll change this according to your needs.

Example Job Description

Position Title: Housekeeper (Cleaner, Gardener, etc.)
Location: (Property Address)
Employment Type: Fixed term - Permanent - Full-time - Part-time - Casual - Live in
Salary and Benefits:

Vision

A clean and comfortable home.

Home's Purpose

Relaxing place to unwind from the pressures of the day.

Role Purpose

The Housekeeper maintains a clean, sanitary, comfortable and tidy environment.

Your Health, Abilities, Safety

Good general health, some back issues require minimisation of heavy lifting.

About the Property

The property consists of a 1,500 square foot residence, a separate two car garage and a small storage shed set in one acre of gardens.

The brick residence includes four bedrooms, two bathrooms, study, games room, a combined kitchen, dining and lounge room plus a utility room.

The household consists of two adults, two children and two dogs.

Responsibilities

- Schedule daily and seasonal tasks.
- Household cleaning, plus maintaining fixtures and appliances.
- Coordinating food provision.
- Clothing care and laundry.
- Reviewing and ordering supplies.
- Pay bills, reconcile the household accounts and manage records.
- Coordinate and supervise services and trades.

Knowledge and Experience

- The capacity to plan and produce three healthy meals each day.
- Understanding cleaning products, techniques and methods.
- The physical stamina and mobility to bend, reach, kneel, and push/pull 15 kg (33 lbs).

Competencies

- Ability to maintain a high level of performance with minimal supervision.

Key Tasks

- Perform a variety of cleaning activities such as sweeping, mopping, dusting and polishing.
- Check stock and replace when appropriate.
- Comply with health and safety policy and practices.

Endorsed:
Name:
Title:
Date:

Approved:
Name:
Title:
Date:

Glossary

Deep Work: daily, uninterrupted time focussing on important work, and further developing the ability to do it well.

Dispatching: the process of assigning resources to tasks.

Effective: producing the expected result.

Efficient: functioning with the least wasted effort.

Essentialism: focusing on completing the essential work.

Housekeeping: managing household affairs.

Ideal Day: a time management concept of the perfect working day that takes advantage of your natural high and low energy periods includes time for uninterrupted work, and all your tasks are completed quickly and easily. It's not really possible to achieve, but you plan your normal days according to the Ideal Day template.

Kaizen: activities that continuously improve processes.

Lean: a systematic method of minimising waste without sacrificing productivity. It assumes that the customer will be willing to pay for improvements in value.

Minimally Viable: the smallest possible thing that satisfies demand.

Prioritisation: arranging work in order of importance (most important first).

Outsourcing: hiring a company to perform services previously done in-house.

Pomodoro Technique: a time management method where you work in short bursts interspersed by breaks. The original technique requires setting a timer for 25 minutes, when it goes off, take a five-minute break before resetting the timer and working again. After four cycles (2 hours) take a longer break of 15 - 30 minutes.

Scheduling: a process of arranging and controlling work to optimise productivity and workloads.

Six Sigma: a statistical method for examining processes and developing improvements leading to a more effective and efficient system.

Spending Plan: a spending forecast that helps you decide whether you can afford unplanned spending.

Standard Conditions: the conditions that promote the most efficient process. See also standard operations and standard practices.

Standard Operations: the most efficient process. See also standard conditions and standard practices.

Standard Practice: instructions on implementing the standard conditions and operations to achieve the best result. See also standard conditions and standard operations.

Tickler File: a bring forward system using 12 monthly files and 31 daily files. Activities are filed by month, and at the start of each new month, transferred to the daily files for action. For example, an activity due on August 14 will start in the August file. At the end of July, you'll file the August papers by date (the 14th under 14). If the 14th is the last possible date, you might file it earlier to ensure it's done.

Time Budget: planning and prioritising tasks according to the time available.

Bibliography

Barker, C. Hélène. 1917. *Wanted, a Young Woman to do Housework: business principles applied to housework.* New York: Moffat, Yard & Co.

Beecher, Catherine E. 1848. *A Treatise on Domestic Economy, for the Use of Young Women at Home, and at School.* Revised ed. New York: Harper & Brothers Publishers.

Beeton, Isabella. Reproduced in facsimile 2000. *The Book of Household Management.* London: Cassell & Co.

Blaelock, Alexandria. 2017. *Holistic Personal Finance: How to pay for the life you want.* Melbourne: BlueMere Books.

Cobb, Linda. 2002. *How the Queen Cleans Everything: Handy Advice for a Clean House, Cleaner Laundry, and a Year of Timely Tips.* New York: Atria Books.

Crabb, Annabelle. 2014. *The Wife Drought: Why women need wives, and men need lives.* North Sydney: Ebury Press.

Davenport, Liz. 2001. *Order From Chaos: A six-step plan for organizing yourself, your office, and your life.* New York: Three Rivers Press.

Duhigg, Charles. 2012. *The Power of Habit: Why we do what we do and how to change.* London: Random House.

Frederick, Christine. 1914. *The New Housekeeping: Efficiency studies in home management.* Garden City: Doubleday, Page & Company.

Frederick, Christine. 1923. *Household Engineering: Scientific management in the home.* Chicago: American School of Home Economics.

Gilbert, Elizabeth. 2015. *Big Magic: Creative Living Beyond Fear.* London: Bloomsbury.

Granger, Jennifer. 2013. *Feminine Lost: Why most women are male.* New York: Weinstein Books.

Keller, Gary and Papasan, Jay. 2012. *The One Thing: The surprisingly simple truth behind extraordinary results.* London: John Murray.

Mackenzie, Alec. 1997. 3rd ed. *The Time Trap: The classic book on time management.* New York: AMACOM.

McKeown, Greg. 2014. *Essentialism: The disciplined pursuit of less.* London: Virgin Books.

Morgenstern, Julie. 2004. 2nd ed. *Organizing from the Inside Out: The foolproof system for organizing your home, your office, and your life.* New York: Henry Holt and Company.

Newport, Cal. 2016. *Deep Work: Rules for Focused Success in a Distracted World.* London: Piatkus.

Pink, Daniel. 2018. *When: The scientific secrets of perfect timing.* Melbourne: Text Publishing.

Scott, Jennifer L. 2014. *At Home with Madame Chic: Becoming a connoisseur of daily life.* New York: Simon & Schuster.

Seely, L. 1902. *Mrs Seely's Cookbook: A manual of French and American Cookery with chapters on domestic servants their rights and duties and many other details of household management.* London: The MacMillan Company

Smith, Adam. 2000. 4th ed. *Wealth of Nations.* London: Penguin Books Ltd.

Strasser, Susan. 1982. *Never Done: A history of American housework.* New York: Henry Holt and Company.

Tate, Carson. 2015. *Work Simply: Embracing the power of your personal productivity style.* London: Portfolio Penguin.

Index

Accounts 25
Aunt Katy 93
Bathroom 85
Bedroom 82
Before You Get Home ... 78
Big House
    staffing 16
Buying 79
Case Study
    Aunt Katy 93
    doing the laundry 112
    hand washing dishes 103
    kitchen standard practice 114
Child Care 33
Cleaning 29
    light v deep v spring .. 31
Cockpit Principle 109
Control 41
Cooking 28
    Mrs Patmore 14
    small house 28
Deep Work 94
Definition
    clean 29
    housekeeping 8
    minimally viable 8
    minimally viable housekeeping 9
Dining Room 80
Dispatching 23
Downton Abbey
    Bates 14
    Baxter 14
    Branson 16
    butler 13
    Carson 13
    cook 14
    estate manager 16
    governess 15
    housekeeper 12
    housekeeping 11
    housemaid 14
    Lady Cora 11
    lady's maid 14
    laundress 16
    Miss Smith 14
    Mrs Hughes 12
    Mrs Patmore 14
    nanny 15
    tutor 15
    valet 14
Effectiveness
    deep work 94
    essentialism 94
    prioritisation 95
    the one thing 95
    time budget 96
Efficiency
    kaizen 119
    lean 119
    outsourcing 121
    six sigma 117
    standardisation 100
Essentialism 94
Estate Manager
    Downton Abbey 16
    small house 34
Exercise 52
Expectations 53
Family
    care 32
    room 81
    working at home 135
Friends
    working at home 135

Functional Rooms 84
    bathroom 85
    garden 87
    home office 86
    kitchen 84
    laundry 85
    study
        adult 86
    toilet 86
Garden 87
    maintenance 34
Health 50
    ability 51
    exercise 52
    safety 51
    working at home 134
Home
    bathroom 85
    bedroom 82
    before you get 78
    dining room 80
    family room 81
    functional rooms 84
    garden 87
    home office 86
    kitchen 84
    laundry 85
    living room 80
    lounge room 80
    play room 83
    private rooms 81
    public rooms 80
    sitting room 80
    study
        adult 86
        child 83
    toilet 86
Home Office 86
Home's Purpose 47
Hotel
    attendants 18
    cook 18
    food and beverages ... 18
    housekeeping 17
    managers 18
    staffing 19
Housekeepers
    amateur 10
    Downton Abbey 12
    hotel 17
    job description 92
    Mrs Hughes 12
    professional 9
Housekeeping
    big house 11
    definition 8
    effectiveness 94
    efficiency 117
    expectations 53
    home's purpose 47
    hotel 17
    kids 60
    outfit 40
    outsourcing 62
    pets 61
    philosophical conflicts
        92
    philosophy 91
    safety 51
    self-care 35
    small house 19
    standard conditions . 107
    standard operations . 106
    standard practice 113
    standardisation 105
    vision 47
    you 56
    your abilities 51
    your health 50
    your partner 58
    your purpose 49
Ideal Day 68
    example 69
    Ms Blaelock's 70
Job Description 92
    example 141

Kaizen 119
Kids
   housekeeping 60
Kindergarten Model 108
Kitchen 84
   conditions 115
   operations 114
   practice 117
   standard practice 114
Laundry 33, 85
   doing 112
   Downton Abbey 16
   small house 33
Lean 119
Light v Deep v Spring Cleaning 31
Living Room 80
Lounge Room 80
Mental Health 41
   control 41
Methodology
   effectiveness 94
   efficiency 117
Minimally Viable
   definition 8
Minimally Viable Housekeeping
   definition 9
Occupational Health and Safety 35
Outdoor Space *See* Garden
Outsourcing 62
   efficiency 121
   functional 65
   housekeeping 62
   in-person 63
   live in 63
   live out 64
   professional 65
Personal Protective Equipment 39
   housekeeping outfit ... 40
Pets

care 33
   housekeeping 61
Philosophy 91
   conflicts 92
Physical Fitness 38
Planning 20
   annual 74
   daily 72
   longer-term 75
   major tasks 76
   minor tasks 75
   monthly 73
   quarterly 74
   weekly 73
Play Room 83
Prioritisation 95
Private Rooms 81
   bedroom 82
   family 81
   play 83
   study
      child 83
Public Rooms 80
   dining 80
   living 80
   lounge 80
   sitting 80
Purchasing 24
Record Keeping 27
Relationships
   working at home 134
Right
   environment 41
   tools 40
Risk Management 36
Safety 51
Safety Policy 38
   Scheduling 38
Scheduling 22
   annual 74
   daily 72
   long-term 75
   major tasks 76

monthly 73
quarterly 74
safety policy 38
weekly 73
Self-care 35
control 41
exercise 52
housekeeping outfit ... 40
mental health 41
personal protective equipment 39
physical fitness 38
right environment 41
right tools 40
risk management 36
safety policy 38
scheduling 38
Sitting Room 80
Six Sigma 117
Small House
accounts 25
cleaning 29
cooking 28
dispatching 23
estate management 34
housekeeping 19
planning 20
purchasing 24
record keeping 27
scheduling 22
Staffing
big house 16
hotel 19
Standard Conditions 101
equipment 110
housekeeping 107
layout 108
storage 109
Standard Operations 101
housekeeping 106
Standard Practice 101
housekeeping 113
working at home 129

Standardisation 100
doing the laundry 112
hand washing dishes 103
kitchen standard practice 114
standard conditions . 101
standard operations . 101
standard practice 101
time and motion studies 102
Study
adult 86
child 83
The One Thing 95
Time and Motion Studies 102
hand washing dishes 103
Time Budget 96
Toilet 86
Vehicles 88
Vision 47
home's purpose 47
your purpose 49
Where
bathroom 85
bedroom 82
before you get home . 78
buying 79
dining room 80
family room 81
functional rooms 84
garden 87
home office 86
kitchen 84
laundry 85
living room 80
lounge room 80
play room 83
private rooms 81
public rooms 80
sitting room 80
study
adult 86

child 83
toilet 86
vehicles 88
Working at Home 128
   balance 132
   colleagues 136
   family 135
   friends 135
   health 134
   motivation 128
   relationships 134
   standard practice 129
   you 132
Yard .... *See* Garden

You
   balance 132
   working at home 132
Your
   abilities 51
   health 50
   home's purpose 47
   partner 58
   purpose 49
   safety 51
   vision 47
Your Partner
   housekeeping 58

Author's Note

Thanks for buying my book. If you like, you can send me an email at hello@alexandriablaelock.com and let me know what you thought.

I know you're busy, so I've tried to keep it short. I hope it helps.

For more housekeeping help, visit alexandriablaelock.com/books/minimally-viable-housekeeping/ or my Pinterest Board for other interesting information at pinterest.com.au/alexblaelock/minimally-viable-housekeeping/

For more, visit me at alexandriablaelock.com to:

- read my blog
- sign up for *Letters from my* Library to stay up to date on the development and release of my books. You'll also get research interestingness (that doesn't get to the blog), gossip about my writing life, and the odd special offer.

About the Author

Alexandria Blaelock writes self-help books applying business techniques to personal matters like getting dressed, cleaning house, and feeding your friends.

She also writes short stories, some of them for *Ellery Queen's Mystery Magazine* and *Pulphouse Fiction Magazine*.

As a recovering Project Manager, she's probably too fond of sticking to plan. She lives in a forest because she enjoys birdsong, the scent of gum leaves and the sun on her face.

When not telecommuting to parallel universes from her Melbourne based imagination, she watches K-dramas, talks to animals, and drinks Campari. At the same time.

Discover more at www.alexandriablaelock.com.

www.ingramcontent.com/pod-product-compliance
Lightning Source LLC
Chambersburg PA
CBHW071455080526
44587CB00014B/2116